# NO TIME FOR FEAR

Paul de Gelder has been a clearance diver with the Royal Australian Navy, in one of its elite frontline teams, since 2006. He has been deployed to Indonesia, Malaysia, Singapore and Thailand as a diver, served in operations in East Timor, and has visited the US to talk about his work.

In his spare time Paul loves working out in the gym, surfing, skydiving and any kind of extreme sport. He is planning a return to motorbike riding.

# NO TIME FOR FEAR

## HOW A SHARK ATTACK SURVIVOR BEAT THE ODDS

# PAUL de GELDER
## with Sue Williams

PENGUIN BOOKS

PENGUIN BOOKS

UK | USA | Canada | Ireland | Australia
India | New Zealand | South Africa | China

Penguin Books is part of the Penguin Random House group of companies
whose addresses can be found at global.penguinrandomhouse.com.

Penguin
Random House
Australia

First published by Penguin Group (Australia), 2011
This edition published by Penguin Group (Australia), 2012

Cover design by Alex Ross © Penguin Group (Australia)
Text design by Marina Messiha © Penguin Group (Australia)
Cover photograph by Tim Bauer ©, courtesy of *Australian Women's Weekly*
Typeset in Fairfield by Post Pre-press Group, Brisbane, Queensland
Printed and bound in Australia by Griffin Press

National Library of Australia
Cataloguing-in-Publication data:

Gelder, Paul de.
No time for fear: how a shark attack survivor beat the odds / Paul de Gelder.
9780143567325 (pbk.)
Gelder, Paul de.
Australia. Royal Australian Navy. Clearance Diving Branch.
Divers – Australia – Biography.
Navies – Australia – Amphibious operations.
Shark attacks – New South Wales – Anecdotes.

359.984

penguin.com.au

This book is dedicated to those who put the freedom of others first and their own safety second. Those who don't ask for thanks, only support, and who travel far from their families and loved ones to take risks so that others can feel safe at home:

the men and women of our defence force.

# CONTENTS

# PROLOGUE

Early one morning on a dark, overcast day in February 2009 in the coolest summer in 50 years, I was taking part in a counter-terrorism exercise in Sydney Harbour.

A Royal Australian Navy clearance diver – from one of the defence force's most elite squads – I was swimming through the water on my back when I felt something smack me hard on the leg.

I rolled over and looked down – straight into the cold black eye of a massive bull shark, one of the most ferocious predators that ever stalked the world's oceans.

I peered closer through the murky water and could see it had something in its massive jaw between its teeth: my leg.

At that moment I knew I was in for the fight of my life.

My first instinct was to slash at the shark's eye but as soon as I went to raise my right hand, I realised I couldn't. The shark had clamped its jaws over my wrist too. I then tried to jab it in the eye with my left hand, but on the angle it was holding me I couldn't reach. Instead, I madly lunged to heave its head off me, but that only served to push the teeth of its lower jaw deeper into my flesh.

Finally, summoning every iota of strength I possessed, I punched it on the nose, as hard as I possibly could.

That seemed to *really* piss it off, and it started shaking me, its teeth working like a saw on my limbs. That's when the pain started. Then it pulled me down under the water. We surfaced back up again together and I gulped for air, not knowing if I'd get another chance. At that moment the shark pulled me under a second time, shaking me again like I was a rag doll. Then it must have lost its grip because suddenly I was free.

When a bull shark attacks, there's usually more than one of them lurking, so I knew I had to get out of the water quickly or I was going to be torn limb from limb and eaten alive.

I couldn't feel my right leg but it wasn't until I started swimming freestyle to get away that I looked up – and saw that my hand was no longer there.

I felt I had no chance of getting out of the water alive, but I was determined that this bastard wouldn't finish me off. All my life I'd been getting into trouble and then out of it again, living the infantry's mantra: improvise, adapt and overcome.

For years, those three simple words had helped push me through some of the toughest challenges I could ever have imagined. And after staring death – with its hungry eyes and razor-sharp teeth – in the face, I was as sure as hell not going to give up on it now . . .

# PART ONE

# IMPROVISE

# 1

# THE HIGH PRICE OF ADVENTURE

All my life I've never looked for trouble, but trouble always seems to find me.

It started when I was a kid. It shouldn't have. My dad, after all, was a policeman. My grandfather was a soldier in World War Two. And, before him, my great-grandfather served in the British forces in World War One.

That long tradition of discipline and courage under fire should have made me the perfectly behaved eldest son my parents were hoping for. But somehow they ended up with a boy who never seemed to do anything right. I was constantly having to be patched up after accidents or fights and I slowly graduated to more and more serious trouble.

From the day I was born in March 1977, I created havoc. My mum, Pat, was in labour with me for 24 hours, and even then

I was so reluctant to enter the world I had to be dragged out by the head with forceps. She said it was such a horrendous birth, she hadn't known what had hit her, and couldn't stand up or sit down for two weeks afterwards. Just as she began to recover, she was whisked back into hospital with a potentially fatal dose of septicaemia.

When she finally got home, she vowed not to have any more children. My dad, Steve, had other ideas, and they ended up having three more: Travis, two years later; Sean, 14 months after that and then, at last, my little sister, Jacqui, four years on.

I wasn't a bad baby though. I slept well and was generally happy and smiley. Looking back, I think I may have my grandmother Betty to thank for that. She often looked after me and – as a product of the British wartime airforce – she'd insist on dipping my dummy into a glass of brandy to help me sleep.

The family started out living in a unit, then a house, in Mornington, a seaside town overlooking Port Phillip Bay on the neck of Victoria's Mornington Peninsula. These days everyone thinks of the area as incredibly scenic with great vineyards and a magnificent racecourse nearby, but the best thing about living there for me was having a hospital right across the road from our house. If they'd had frequent-visitor points, I would have been the one leaving with the free set of steak knives. Maybe it was lucky they didn't. Odds on I would have managed immediately to impale myself while practising my swordplay.

I was a high-spirited, physically adventurous kid, far too daring for my own good. I loved my skateboard and I'd ride it up and down for hours, sometimes grabbing on to the back of someone's bike – or car – to catch a tow. Mum was always getting calls from the hospital to let her know I was in there again after falling off, or being knocked out, and ending up cut, broken and bruised.

Even at home I was no safer. At the age of four I was playing football in the backyard with a friend when I leapt up for the ball, tripped over and cracked my head against the Hills Hoist. Instantly I was covered in blood, with more gushing out all the time, like a fully open tap. The minute Mum saw me she screamed louder than I'd ever heard anyone scream before. I had a hole in my head, she said later, the size of a fist. She wrapped me in a towel and raced me to hospital. The doctor thought I'd fractured my skull and to check he took a pair of steel scissors, put them inside the hole and rubbed them across the bone to see if they'd catch. It hurt like hell. Happily, he ruled a fracture out then stitched me up beautifully.

Two years later I had my nose bitten off. I was playing outside the health centre Mum was visiting when I noticed a dog on the back porch. I've always loved dogs and went straight over and started patting it. When I finally gave the dog a big hug goodbye, it gave my face an almighty chomp.

I barged into the health centre yelling, again covered in blood, and this time holding my nose onto my face. When the people sitting in the waiting room saw me, they all started screaming. Hearing the commotion, and fearful it might have something to do with me, Mum poked her head round the door of the consulting room and went white. She grabbed me and took me to the hospital, sobbing all the way.

'Don't worry,' I somehow found the strength to tell her. 'It'll be all right!' And, sure enough, it was. I ended up with 18 stitches to my face and a nose that never looked quite the same again, but I was generally none the worse for wear. It set up a pattern that was to continue for many years to come: the mad escapades, the injuries and consoling my mum, reassuring her that I'd survive, no matter what.

Gradually, I learned to work out risk and measure the dangers a bit more carefully. I stayed away from the pointy end of animals, mostly. I practised my skateboarding skills so I'd fall off less often. And I learned to stay on my feet a bit more when I played football.

Of course, I was still the ringleader who directed my kid brothers and sister to do crazy things – like jump from the roof of the house into the pool or line up the trampoline so we could spring off it into the water, but I slowly learned to try to make sure I wouldn't get too hurt. After all, you could live your life cushioned in cottonwool, never taking a risk, never doing, seeing or experiencing anything exciting, and stay as safe as houses. But that didn't sound like any fun at all.

I was always seeking thrills and wasn't scared of anything. When you're young, you feel you have nothing to be scared of anyway. You have no idea how bad things can really be. These days, I'm not that different. I just try not to think about the fact I could die doing something, and then I do it anyway.

I'll throw myself wholeheartedly into every situation, hoping for the best and never even thinking about the worst. Why would you? I was always determined to live life to the fullest and was confident that even if things did get crazy along the way, I could cope with whatever was thrown at me.

I believe it's important to aim high rather than settling for the safe second-best option. You see people all the time who've bubble-wrapped themselves, who never want to try anything different or new, who seem scared of *really* living. But there's just so much to see and do – why limit yourself because of fear?

Already, even at a young age, I knew adventure was out there, but I didn't know there was sometimes a high price to pay.

# 2.

# A LOVE AFFAIR WITH THE SEA

I grew up loving the sea – but I was always scared of sharks. Always. Being in the sea is to my mind the closest anyone can get to being part of nature. And sharks are an ominous reminder of how brutal and unforgiving nature can really be.

As a young kid I'd seen the 1975 movie *Jaws*, about the great white shark menacing a US coastal town. Along with everyone else I'd been hesitant to go back in the water again. Then I saw the 1978 film *Piranha*, the comedy-horror flick about a swarm of killer piranhas, and that scared me even more. The part when the two teenagers skinny-dip in the pool and are attacked, vanishing under the water, made me shudder even thinking about it.

I often thought about sharks, and sometimes killer piranhas, when I went into the ocean, but my love of the water always overcame my fears. Whether you're swimming, surfing, diving or even paddling, there's a real connection to the natural environment, and it's incredibly grounding. When you're going through good times in your life, it adds an extra dimension to how you feel. When you're going through tough times, it has the capacity to wash away the stresses, calm you down and make you feel better about everything. And even in my darkest days I've found taking time out for a quick dip has the power to make everything seem easier to handle.

That passion for the ocean runs through all the generations of our family. Dad was a champion swimmer in his youth and chose to live in Mornington because it was on the sea. Working as a policeman in nearby Frankston, he continued his swimming and won a lot of medals in police swimming comps, setting quite a few records here and there. He was determined that all his kids would be able to swim from an early age. One by one when we were just babies, he'd take us down to the local pool and give us our first swimming lesson. In my case I was two weeks old. Apparently, I loved it from the very first moment I felt the water close over my head and I gurgled as I came back up.

Dad taught others to swim too. He started a swimming squad in Frankston, which became the biggest and strongest in the area. It even had a waiting list. When I got older, I'd jump out of bed before dawn a few times a week and go with him, and often join him after school too. It didn't take long until I was one of the best swimmers there.

Dad comes from a long line of sea-faring wanderers. My great-grandfather Adrian de Gelder was born in Amsterdam in the Netherlands but crossed the sea to the US and settled there for a period, before setting sail over the Pacific Ocean to show up in Australia. He was a bit of a chancer who liked to try his luck. The family story is that his birth was never officially registered, allowing him to live tax-free his whole life. But his luck didn't always hold. In 1939 he bought a ticket in a Tatts draw for the Melbourne Cup and ended up with a horse called Old Rowley. That year it ran last. The next year he chose to back a different horse. Unfortunately, this time Old Rowley, at odds of 100–1, won the Cup – one of only three horses with such long odds ever to have done so.

When the eldest of his children, Wally – my dad's dad – hit his teens, Adrian suddenly took off again, leaving his son to support the whole family. To earn money Wally joined the Australian Merchant Navy, shipping troops and supplies around the world and sometimes directly supporting World War Two military operations. It was dangerous work. Merchant seamen suffered some of the highest casualty rates of the war from German U-boats. They often had heavy losses against enemy aircraft too, and many of them died running supplies to Russian ports in the freezing waters. They were also among the first Australians captured by enemy forces as they often sailed without an escort, and proved easy prey to Japanese raiders and air attacks.

Wally came a cropper when his ship was torpedoed and sank somewhere off the coast of New Guinea. He and other survivors spent a couple of days in shark-infested waters before being picked up by an American warship. He served out the rest of the war on that ship as a cook, and received a medal from the Americans for his service.

Funnily enough, Wally, the eldest of seven, ended up marrying the youngest of another family of seven, Molly, the daughter of a butcher at Menzies, just outside Kalgoorlie. She was a similarly adventurous type. She joined the Australian Airforce and on one occasion was made to travel from Perth to Melbourne by ship through waters that at the time were classified as part of the war zone. As a result of that trip she was considered a war veteran, and received a pension for the rest of her life. She was always grateful to the sea for that!

My grandparents on my mum's side were in the British forces during World War Two. My grandmother Betty was in the airforce, and my grandfather Jim was conscripted into the army to man the anti-aircraft guns and was dropped behind enemy lines in Germany. Afterwards, he worked as a bus driver, then as an ambulance driver, but could never settle down. He longed for adventure and so in 1963, when my mum was ten years old, the family set sail for Australia as ten-pound Poms.

They decided to try their luck in Melbourne, but as migrants it was tough finding jobs. They both ended up in a factory, with Betty doing an assortment of cleaning jobs on the side. It was a hard adjustment to make. The first summer they were here was unbelievably hot and apparently my grandmother would sit and cry because she hated it so much. They didn't have the money to go home so she decided there was no alternative but to get on with it.

My British grandparents moved around a bit and ended up in Dandenong, 30 kilometres southeast of the centre of Melbourne. My mum had wanted to be a nurse but the family weren't well off, so she left school at 15 to go to work and earn some money, getting a job in the postal service. She met my dad, Steve, at the engagement party for her sister, who was marrying the son of a policeman. Dad was an officer at the same station.

Mum was 18 when she married Dad, who was four years older, in 1972. They spent a bit of time having a typical de Gelder wander around Australia, then settled in Mornington. I was born at the hospital in Frankston five years later and named Paul after Nanny Betty's eldest son – Mum's brother – who died of bronchiolitis when he was just five months old.

At first I was a good boy, the perfect son. As the eldest, I think Mum came to depend on me to help with the other kids. It made me grow up fast. At just three and a half I was looking after my youngest brother, Sean. At eight, I had my sister to babysit too. I vividly remember putting her in the pram and walking Jacqui up and down the street – although I also remember stealing her nappies, tying them around my neck and running around, pretending to be Superman.

It might have been that defence forces background and their own strict upbringings, coupled with Dad's work in the police, but my parents were actually very tough on us. Dad was often away, or doing shiftwork, so it was left to Mum to discipline three unruly boys, and a girl doing her best to be just like us. It can't have been easy.

She did it probably the only way she knew how: by running the house like a regimental sergeant-major who'd got out of the wrong side of bed, hit his head, and then stubbed his toe on the bedpost. The military had nothing on her. We were making our own beds and tidying our shared bedrooms almost from the moment we could stand on two legs. Everything had to be spotless. She'd get angry with us if we didn't do something, or did something wrong, but she could never scare us into doing the right thing. She'd take away our pocket money or ground us or, like parents did in those days, hit us with a wooden spoon. She broke so many she graduated to those hard rubber ones. They hurt much more, but we usually deserved it. And she still couldn't tame me.

It would take a bit to get Dad riled up but we copped a fair few beatings from him too. If he slid that belt off his trousers, you'd start crying immediately. Your knees would buckle even before he got to you. He was over six foot tall and strong, with big shoulders. He'd pick you up by one arm, and flog you as you dangled. Unlike with Mum I was scared enough of him to do whatever he said – and usually pretty quickly too.

He was at work a lot and loved being part of the police force. He didn't talk about it much, though. I remember just before Christmas one year when I was very young, huddled with my brothers and Mum by the front door while a huge storm raged outside. All the lights suddenly blew. Mum was freaking out, especially as Dad was working at the time. I found out later that he'd been hunting a gunman who'd shot his mother after an argument with his father, and then shot five other people on the street. Dad, together with his police partner, had found a witness and took him for a drive around the streets to try to spot the man. When they found him, the killer raised the gun to my dad but just before he could fire, the partner shot him. The gunman died while Dad tried to render first aid. For that, Dad won the Chief Commissioner's Certificate.

Another time a 17-year-old boy heard a rumour that his brother had been beaten up in jail, so he went on a rampage. The claims weren't true but he didn't know that, and he climbed onto a roof with a shotgun, and started shooting at houses and cars up and down the street. Dad got to the scene, found a way onto the property and started talking to him from the front yard. It was very dangerous – the kid could easily have shot him. He did fire a few more times over the next four hours, but happily not at Dad. It all got too risky because of his mood swings and Dad was ordered to get out of the line of fire while a SWAT team moved in.

Eventually, the kid agreed to surrender . . . but only to Dad. He went to the side of the roof, and Dad had to come back out in full view of him. The kid then handed him the firearm and came down. Dad was highly commended by the force for his actions. Over the next few years he was involved in another two firearm incidents. In the second, a potential siege situation, he actually found the offender asleep in his car with the firearm. For a while the other police officers started calling him 'the siege man'. To us he seemed fearless.

But he just didn't talk about that side of his life to us kids. I think he felt that if you wanted to be a normal person in life, you had to move all the distasteful things that you'd witnessed or experienced to a secret, hidden place, and not let them come out too often. We're probably not that different.

As the eldest child, whenever I had time off from my chores of looking after my siblings, I managed to claim a fair bit of freedom.

At every opportunity I'd slip out to play with my mates or ride my BMX bike up to the track 2 kilometres away, even though I was meant to be confined to the street just outside the house. I'd swear I'd been there the whole time.

That combination of early independence and a super-strict regime at home, however, was explosive. Gradually, I became more and more frustrated and irritated by all the rules. Later that would turn me into a real rebel, never happier than when I was slipping out of the house to meet up with friends and getting into more and more mischief.

But back then I found escape in the ocean, swimming and mucking about in the shallows. We lived near a number of beaches at Mornington, both quiet, sandy spots and others great for surfing. The rips could sometimes be treacherous, but I remember Dad having such confidence in our swimming abilities that he would let us go out into huge swells with our boogie boards, although he did have to rescue Sean once or twice and haul him back to land.

My best times at the beach, however, were always with my favourite grandad, Wally. He lived in Carrum, about 20 kilometres north of our place, and I really loved spending time with him. He was a huge, hulking man who'd take me out spearfishing in the ocean. I'd squeeze into an tiny old wetsuit that had once belonged to an aunt or uncle when they were kids. To get it on I'd have to put my feet in plastic bags to enable them to slide in, and sprinkle talcum powder all over myself before yanking it on over my body. Then, standing on the beach, Grandad Wally would hand over a speargun so big it was too heavy for me, still a tiny skinny kid, to cock alone, and we'd half wade, half swim out to the reef and try to spear flathead and stingrays. I loved it, and he was my hero for making it happen. I felt really at home in the water and enjoyed the rush of hunting.

It always felt safe with him by my side. There was the idle worry about whether there might be sharks around but with my grandad there I always felt protected, as if nothing could get me. Mind you, I'd often become engrossed in the hunting and it'd be a while before I finally looked up to see where he was. Many times he'd be nowhere in sight. Then I'd discover he'd gone back to the beach, to the other side of the point, which was a designated nudist spot. He'd be chatting to a couple of naked women, having left me, assured of my swimming skills, out there completely alone.

At other times he'd take us to the nearby Patterson River, blow up an old rubber raft and float it, with us kids on board, down into a creek. From there we'd row to the mouth of the ocean with him walking on the shore alongside to make sure we didn't drown. Often we'd also go walking on the beach with him and he'd chat up women he came across along the way. He was a real free spirit, adventurous and great fun. I idolised him.

Once he took me down to Flinders Beach in the national park, where there was a huge rock face, heaps of weeds, and fish to spear. We spent hours there mucking about in the shallows, then swimming further and further out to where the sea was so deep and dark you had no idea what was lurking beneath you.

Many years later I was on a small-arms training course with the navy, learning to aim and shoot with huge 50-calibre machine-guns. We'd lean back to balance, then fire them at windsocks dragged along by planes. I was crouched down, looking out over the cliff nearby when I thought, *Jeez, that beach looks familiar!* I asked someone the name of where we were, and it was where I used to go spearfishing with Grandad.

One of the guys with me looked horrified when he heard.

'You're joking!' he said. 'You used to spearfish off that point? Didn't you know there's been a huge colony of great whites living there for years?'

That was Grandad. He didn't have too much time for worrying about what might happen, what dangers might be waiting for you. He was too busy living for the moment. I hoped that one day I'd be just like him.

# 3

## TAKING CRAP

These days I'm fit and strong and hard, and I don't take crap from anyone. I've had years of working at it, having it drilled into me by the defence forces. I like being in complete control of my life. But as a kid it wasn't that way at all. And I'm sure that's one of the reasons I'm the way I am now.

While I'd been so fiercely independent, at school I started having difficulties. At home I was the oldest and biggest but compared to other kids my age I was small and skinny – the perfect target for bullies. It was probably all the swim training I was doing that left me so weedy and unable to pack on any extra weight. We never seemed to have enough food at home either. Mum knew how to stretch the budget: we'd always have the scraggiest bits of meat and the parts of animals no one else wanted to eat, like sheep's brains, but I remember always being hungry. Feeding four growing children, keeping a roof over our heads and running a car on a cop's wage can't have been easy.

We moved a lot with Dad's job and so it always felt like I was the new boy at school, the one who stood out. My first school had been Mornington's St Macartan's, a strict Catholic school run by nuns. Then when I was nine, we moved to Frankston and I started at St John's. The school had a composite class for years 4 and 5. There the littler kids got picked on by the bigger ones and, as one of the weediest, I got the full brunt of the bullying. The kids laughed at the way I always wore second-hand clothes from the school op shop, or hand-me-downs, or improvised clothes that Mum had made. Instead of cool blue or white Dunlops, I had old brown ones that did up with two Velcro straps.

Even worse, I'd just finished Year 4 at my last school, but my parents didn't think I was old enough to go into Year 5 yet, so I ended up doing a full two years in that class. As well as being puny, I was also pretty reserved and didn't stand up for myself. I didn't know how to. I didn't have much confidence and I didn't know how to fight. I just kept trudging along, trying to keep my head down. You learned to get on with it; that was life. I was teased and called names and pushed and shoved and bashed a bit, but I just tried to keep away from the bullies and protect my younger brothers, who were also targets.

Even the prospect of getting to know girls offered little distraction. At that age the girls were bigger than many of us boys, and much tougher. In truth I was a bit scared of them. In the playground it wasn't catch-and-kiss we played, with girls versus boys. It was usually catch-and-deck, and I always came off the worse. But there was one girl who was keen on me. She actually had her friend lock us in the sports-room closet and I wasn't allowed out until I kissed her. It was my first ever kiss.

We'd bought our first house there and it was a lot nicer than the old rented one. But shortly afterwards, in July 1989, interest rates shot up to the all-time high of 17 per cent and with it came the recession 'we had to have'. There was a lot of tension and arguments between Mum and Dad, and I think our financial situation had a lot to do with it.

At that time I quite liked learning, and I particularly enjoyed writing and drawing and seemed to have a natural flair for languages. I was always at least a B student and every single report said I just needed to pay a bit more attention. I never liked team sports and I hated football since I didn't have any padding on my skinny legs and knobbly knees, and it hurt being roughed up. That must have been a huge embarrassment for my dad, who coached junior Australian Rules teams and was my football coach for a time. But, happily, he could take some satisfaction from my swimming and long-distance running. I loved swim comps and walked away with all sorts of age championship trophies and ribbons. My parents kept scrapbooks of all my wins.

Shortly after our move Dad was seconded with the police to Brisbane, and six months later he was posted to the Australian Bureau of Criminal Intelligence – now the Australian Crime Commission – in Canberra to represent Victoria on national intelligence projects and drug-offence recording systems. We rented out our house and moved up to Canberra. This time it wasn't only a new place to live and go to school, but a whole new part of Australia.

We lived in Barton first, a suburb near Capital Hill full of government buildings, then Deakin in south Canberra – just around the corner from where Colin Winchester, the assistant commissioner in the Australian Federal Police, was assassinated in January 1989 in the driveway of his house. That was a huge case at the time, and it had a big impact on all the police, including Dad. He became even busier with his job and, apart from taking me swimming, even less involved in my life.

I dreaded starting at my new school, St Benedict's, and wondered if I'd be bullied there too. I still remember my first day. As I walked through the gates there was a big crowd of kids standing there waiting. My heart sank until I realised they were all smiling at me – they'd actually turned out to welcome the new kid! It was a very small school by comparison with St John's, only 130 pupils, and had very small classes. I was a real novelty, and I could hardly believe the warmth of that welcome. One of the first boys I met at that school was a kid called Brock, who became a lifelong friend. I loved going round to his house. His dad was a cop too, but his family all seemed to get on and there you could eat what you wanted. They seemed to talk to each other, and had a laugh. I started to spend more and more time at his place. At school I got along with nearly everyone and even ended up becoming vice-captain of the school in Year 6, although I don't think they actually had many kids to choose from . . .

In my spare time I was still sneaking out to ride skateboards, bikes or just hang out with my new friends. I was still very adventurous – and accident-prone. One evening I must have fallen off my skateboard as I was found face down in a pool of my own blood near the local shops. The first I knew of it was when I woke up in an ambulance on the way to hospital, with ambulance officers asking me questions and trying to find out how they could get in touch with my family. For a while, I had a face full of scabs but, to this day, I have no idea what happened.

I started playing up in other ways too. We were brought up going to church every single Sunday, rain, hail or shine, and being bored with mass, I decided to become an altar boy. It was far more interesting to pour wine and ring bells than to listen to the priest every week. One Sunday as I was getting changed out the back, I heard the *ching-ching* of someone putting money in the poor box. The temptation was just too much and I stole $2. After church Mum and Dad took my brothers to football training, and I got my skateboard, rode up to the shops, bought a block of Top Deck and came home to eat it in front of *Video Hits*. I had the same routine for a few weeks.

God got me back, though. Not only did He ruin chocolate for me, but the whole dairy section. As a teenager, I discovered I was lactose-intolerant – unlike the rest of my family – and from that moment on eating chocolate, ice-cream, yoghurt or anything containing milk gave me huge painful stomach cramps for hours afterwards. It took 15 years for Him to forgive me, by putting Lacteeze tablets on the market, enabling people like me to eat dairy products in comfort for about an hour after taking a pill.

It wasn't long before we were back on the move, and next we went to the south Canberra suburb of Red Hill. I changed schools again, starting Year 7 at St Edmund's College, a much bigger school this time, run by the Christian Brothers. In Year 7 alone there were more than 100 kids. The good thing was that I could now walk to school, rather than catching a bus, and I'd collect my new mates along the way. The bad thing about the school was how incredibly disciplinarian it was.

To a high-spirited kid it felt like jail. There were rules about everything: when you could speak, when you couldn't; what you should wear, what you couldn't; what you should say; how you should behave. It was absolutely stifling. What's more, it was very rugby-oriented – the St Eddie's team had won the Waratah Shield, Union's NSW and, back then, the ACT high-school comp, more than any other school. Past students included former Wallabies captain George Gregan and Matt Giteau as well as League's Ricky Stuart, Luke Priddis and David Furner. Naturally, I didn't fit into the football teams too well. Indeed, I was so shit that often I didn't even get up off the bench during games. And no one was backwards in letting me know what they thought of me.

All these pressures were starting to get on top of me. I basically hated being a teenager, absolutely hated it. I guess it all came down to finding your feet in the world, your identity. Although I had some good friends by now, I was miserable at school. The discipline was unrelenting and the bullies were getting me down both in and outside school. I'd started a paper round that I did on my skateboard, making about $2 an hour, which felt like a fortune. One day I ran into a neighbourhood bully who ended up punching me in the face. I dumped the rest of the newspapers, went home in tears and packed in the job.

At home Mum was stressed out by even more money worries. She and Dad, as Catholics, were determined to send us to

Catholic school and, despite having to scrimp and save to pay our school fees, even with the discounts she got from having three boys, we were often behind in the payments. As well, she had all the pressures that come with bringing up four kids and keeping her marriage together. She was much tougher on me than the younger kids, and it felt as though she was really trying to control my life. It was all rules with her. I felt I could barely move, either at home or at school, without being told what I had to do – and what I couldn't. I just really wanted to be left alone to live my life.

And that's when I started cutting myself.

# 4

# FIGHTING FOR MY LIFE

I think a lot of teenagers have suicidal thoughts. They can enter your head for all sorts of reasons and in all kinds of circumstances. In my case I hated life; I hated everything. The whole adolescent-hormone crap was messing up my whole system. Some kids cope with it. I didn't.

I longed for some kind of escape, but I'd been brought up a Catholic. Even though faith was never really a big part of my life, I did believe in God and Heaven and Hell. Aside from *Piranha* and *Jaws*, *The Exorcist* movies were the scariest I'd ever seen. So killing myself would be like throwing God's gift of life back in His face, and I'd go to Hell for it. And that didn't seem a particularly attractive option.

Instead I'd sit in my bedroom with a hobby knife and slowly cut my arms, watching the dark blood trickle down my skin.

I don't know why I did it. I just knew I had all this aggression and pain inside and somehow I had to get it out. And that seemed to be a way. It was stupid, but how do you rationalise it? I had all this anger and it was easiest to inflict it on myself. The knife wasn't very sharp, so the cuts were incredibly painful and the gashes pretty messy. I'd clean myself up afterwards, staring at all that blood running down the drain in the bathroom, careful never to get any on my clothes. I was able to keep it secret, so my parents never suspected and only a few of my friends ever knew.

The pain somehow gave me solace. I know it sounds bizarre but it felt like a relief. It made me feel alive. At that point what saved me was that I started trying to wrest back some control over my life.

At St Edmund's I'd become good mates with a boy I'd first met at St Benedict's, Steven Dalla Costa, Dalla for short. We both used to hang out at Manuka Pool, a beautiful old art deco outdoor place, over the summer. During the winter, I used to hate that pool for all those before-school training sessions, but in the warmer months it became a refuge for all the kids from the surrounding neighbourhoods. Dalla wasn't a great swimmer but he was awesome on the springboard. We'd get on it and try all sorts of dives: backflips, somersaults, everything. Some of the TV crews would come down to take footage of us mucking around to herald the start of summer each year in their news bulletins. We broke that springboard so many times bouncing on it to help each other get more height, they eventually removed it altogether.

We quickly formed a strong friendship and pretty soon were inseparable. He even thought I was cool – he hadn't tried skateboarding before, and he liked the way I had different clothes to everyone else. Mum made our hoodies and pants to save money; she'd always ask us which colour we wanted the sleeves and the hoods, so they'd end up all different. When Dalla and I found out that we only lived five minutes away from each other, we'd meet every day in a laneway halfway between our houses and walk to school together – we'd always be late! – and then back again afterwards. When we each got home, we'd change before meeting up again to go to the pool or play a couple of hours of basketball. After dark we'd hang around in the laneway just talking. Neither of us wanted to go home; Dalla's dad was from an old-fashioned Italian background and was even stricter than mine.

Dalla was a bit bigger than me, but still weedy, and he was also having a lot of trouble with bullies. One day the biggest bully in our schoolyard knocked all the books out of his hands, called him names and told him he'd meet him later at the bus stop for a fight. Dalla obediently went along at the appointed time . . . and had the crap beaten out of him. It felt like the last straw.

His older brothers' friends were doing Muay Thai kickboxing at a place called Angel Martial Arts, so we asked if we could go along. That was to be a turning point in my life; it changed everything. We were 16 and, suddenly, we were learning how to fight. We got stronger and tougher. With most martial arts you learn about control, restraint and how to stop fights. But there it was all about fighting tools and tactics, how to knock people out and improvise defences. There was no spirituality, no theory. You were being trained, pure and simple, to win fights.

Muay Thai is sometimes known as 'the science of eight limbs' because it uses each point of your body as a weapon – your fists, elbows, shins, knees and even your head. In the lessons you'd kick, punch, elbow and knee your partner in the stomach and legs until they couldn't take it any more, and then swap places. You'd stand there with your hands on your head while your partner kicked you all over, then hammered at your stomach. They called it 'conditioning'. The aim was to make you stronger and harder so you wouldn't feel it so much if people punched you. You'd come out bruised, battered and bloodied but on top of the world: no one was going to be able to kick you around any more.

I found I loved the physicality of learning to fight, the competitiveness of it all and becoming more tolerant of pain. I pushed myself harder and harder because I knew I was getting stronger all the time, and developing my mental toughness. I just got so much out of it. I enjoyed the confidence it gave me. I'd push Dalla and he'd push me, and as soon as we finished school each day we'd turn up to training early and give it everything we had. We suddenly knew how to hit people and make them go down so they couldn't get up for a while. It felt great. That time also coincided with a bit of a growth spurt in both of us. Then a whole bunch of us got together in my backyard one weekend and we all shaved our heads together. It made us look as tough as we were beginning to feel inside.

One day while I was shooting hoops in the school gym, a mate ran up to me and said that someone called my mum a 'fucking slut' in the tuckshop where she was working. I had my own issues with my mum, but I definitely didn't like anyone else having a go. I knew who the boy was, knew that he was a bit of a bully and decided to go and get him. On the way I bumped into Dalla and he joined me.

When I saw the guy, I went over to him and asked him what he'd said about my mum. He told me, so I pushed him. He tried to punch me and I elbowed him so hard he spun a full 360 degrees and crumpled to the ground, unconscious. He came to soon after, but never came near us again. In fact, no one touched us after that. Word spread fast and soon we got a bit of a reputation, whether we deserved it or not.

It felt so good to have some control over our existence. The world was a different place. And we started going out and fighting a lot. A real lot.

### Steve Dalla Costa (Dalla), friend

When we used to go kickboxing together, Paul pushed himself to train hard because he was getting something back from it. He was learning self-control for the first time, and the mental toughness you need to be able to fight back. I guess it was a reflection of our lives at the time as well – us getting into a little more trouble and fighting and so on. We both knew that if we wanted to get bigger and better (and remain safe), we needed to put the time into training hard. We had a goal.

At that time there was a lot of fighting on the streets of Canberra at night. Everyone was doing it. There were only two places to go in those days – Civic, the city centre, or Woden, the other town centre – and on Friday and Saturday nights lots of people would spill out of the clubs drunk, and schoolkids would arrive

NO TIME FOR FEAR

from drinking on street corners, and everyone would be looking for excitement. Some statistic came out at the time saying the ACT had the highest rate of assaults per capita in the whole of Australia. You could see why. There were whole groups of kids going out and fighting, as well as all these ethnic groups, like Tongans, Macedonians, Indians, Serbs, Croats, Aboriginal kids . . . Everyone would be just spoiling for some action. You would go out and see these great drunken brawls rolling down the street, and at least two or three smaller fights at surrounding bus stops.

Now we felt like fighters, we'd go out fighting every Friday and Saturday night. A few of you would be walking along, you'd bump shoulders with a few of another group, no one would back down and suddenly it'd be on. Late at night we'd sneak home with blood all over our shirts and jeans – sometimes your blood, sometimes someone else's. Mum was always puzzled but I'd explain it away as an accident. To me and my mates it was a badge of honour. We were proud of it. Looking back, the whole thing was bloody stupid, but it was almost a rite of passage in our world. And after a few months of fighting I stopped cutting myself. I'd found a completely different release for all the teenage testosterone coursing through my body. If I hadn't learnt how to fight and continued cutting myself instead, who knows what might have happened to me.

The fighting in many ways almost seemed safer. No one ever used weapons like they do today. I remember one night, in the middle of a brawl, someone pulled out a knife. Everyone stopped fighting immediately and just looked at him. *Whoa!* No one wanted to go there.

Because we'd both been bullied so much, Dalla and I never picked on nice kids or ones who were smaller than us. One night when we'd snuck, underage, into a club, Dalla saw a guy who used to beat him up regularly at school. We went up to him and Dalla asked if he could buy him a drink. The guy just looked at him, shook his head and vanished out the back way. His girlfriend said he was scared and thought we'd been taking the piss. So Dalla followed him to another bar, bought him a drink and they ended up becoming friends. It was him saying, 'You don't have power over me any more.' Everyone knew it, but this was Dalla showing he wasn't afraid to approach someone who'd done him wrong. Dalla was always ahead of me on ethics – I was always keener to beat up the people who'd attacked me – but we both learnt a valuable lesson that night. People can change, and I could change too.

The fights were all usually fuelled by alcohol. I'd meet my mates, Dalla, Robbo, Lez, Matt and a few others, and we'd hang out drinking cheap wine, either flavoured Passion Pop or cask wine, which we called 'goonie bags'. Whenever my parents got suspicious, saying I smelled of alcohol or cigarettes, I said I was with some other people who were drinking and smoking. Because they wanted so much to believe me, I think they often did. Besides I was always extra careful to keep Dad in the dark; I knew with his police background he could all too easily put the clues together to work out what I was up to.

### Steve de Gelder, dad

As an infant, boy and teenager, Paul was simply an average person who learned to pretty much look after himself. As the eldest in the family – as I was the eldest in mine, and my father the eldest before me – you learn to take care of yourself, mostly.

He was average at school, at sport, and a genuinely easy person to be with. He was a good boy, most of the time. As with all of us there were a few regrettable incidents in his life, but mostly he was no trouble. During Paul's teenage years I was travelling a great deal, thus not home to help his mother as much as might be normal for a father. Neither of us was particularly aware of him being in any diabolical trouble. Obviously, he had enough maturity not to cross the line too far.

Dalla's Italian grandfather fermented his own grappa, a fruit brandy made from what was left of grapes after making wine – the skins, pips, stalks and stems. We used to steal bottles and take them to the local memorial gardens to drink. It was amazingly strong. One time we were all blind on it and went along to a party, at the huge fabulous house of some girl whose parents were away. Halfway through the night a few guys turned up and started loading designer clothes from the wardrobes into big bags and then leaving with them. Everyone was so drunk, they all started doing the same. We joined in and went from room to room, looking for stuff to steal – there were watches, stereos, even an air rifle. We piled it all up under a tree in the front yard, meaning to make off with it later. But we were so drunk we forgot all about it.

We did some other stupid things when we'd been drinking. I learned to drive when I was drunk. We'd been to a party and I asked a mate with a car if I could drive it home. He didn't mind.

Looking back, it's amazing none of us – or anyone else – was badly hurt or killed. Why does it seem such a good idea when you've been drinking to suddenly get behind the wheel of a one-tonne missile?

When no one had a car, we'd often just try to break into one in the neighbourhood and drive it home. We'd go from driveway to driveway or around a car park, trying all the car doors to see if any had been left open. And if they were, we'd often also take the stereo, umbrellas, cassette tapes, anything that had been left inside. A couple of times we were spotted and chased by angry owners. But we were young and fast and always managed to get away.

Growing up, I'd always found it hard not having the latest stuff like other kids. Our family just didn't have the money. I found a solution to this too. Some of my friends had weekend or after-school jobs so they could afford new things; I just stole stuff. Suddenly, everything was free, and I could have the things I'd always wanted but could never buy. You needed a razor to start shaving with, so you'd go out and steal the most expensive one you could find. You wanted a new jacket, so you'd go into the nicest store to pick one out. I no longer had to wear those crappy old brown sneakers. Some things you used yourself; others you gave to friends or sold for cash. Dalla and I both did some work experience at a sports store, so when we came home in new gear I think Mum assumed we'd been given it there. But as well as getting things you couldn't afford – and even things you didn't need at all – it was about the challenge of not getting caught. It was the thrill.

Inevitably, however, I was caught, and twice. The first time was when I tried to steal both a Walkman and new batteries to go in it for a trip I was going on. The second time was when I stole a Pierre Cardin tie for a friend who was going to give it to his dad for his birthday. I got clothes-lined by a security guard, completely knocked off my feet and then dragged down the street by my neck. It was so embarrassing. They called my mum but – probably wanting to force me to take responsibility for my own actions – she told them to call the cops. The security guard looked at me hard but I caught a glint in his eye that said, *I feel sorry for you, kid; you've got it bad at home when even your mum won't help!*

He let me off.

I was still going hungry at home, so Dalla and I also started stealing people's lunches from their lockers at school. If just a corner of the locker was open, we'd bend back the aluminium door to get at their sandwiches. We'd go down the lunch line scabbing money too. We weren't doing much else at school, really. We were just impatient for each schoolday to finish so we could go and hang out.

With the money I got from selling knocked-off gear, I also started smoking dope and doing even more stupid things, like sucking on soda bulbs for the nitrous oxide. That was really dumb, like sniffing paint. But it was the hardest we ever went. There just weren't many harder drugs around at that time in our circles. Weed was our main thing. We'd be going into the dodgiest of apartment blocks, where we'd knock on a door and someone would open it just a crack to ask you what you wanted, go away and then come back and slip you the gear. At one house we went to, the young woman inside asked us to watch her kids for ten minutes while she went out. We were so stunned, we did. Another time a woman sent one of her children to the bedroom to get us what we wanted. *Hang on!* we thought to ourselves. *You can't do that! That's not good parenting!* But we went back later all the same.

My relationships with my friends grew stronger and stronger and I didn't want to be at home and around my parents any more. There wasn't a lot of communication in our house anyway, unless it was Mum or Dad yelling at each other, or at me. Dad didn't play an active role in my teenage years, and he spent a lot of time out working different shifts. Mum often seemed at the end of her tether, trying to cope with four kids on a single wage. Spending time with my mates felt so much more comfortable and simpler. As a result those friendships became the most important things in my life, and those guys are my best friends to this day. We were always there for each other for company and guidance, and it really felt like we understood each other. Besides them, the only other thing that mattered was martial arts.

Apart from learning to fight, it was also about being physical and getting fit. Martial arts challenged me all the time. Looking back, I would have loved to have known how to look after myself at a younger age. Martial arts, when it's taught properly and is not just about beating up the next kid, can build any child a good base for the rest of their lives. It can teach you how to *stop* fights, with grappling and getting people into submission holds, rather than just getting stuck into the hitting and kicking. And the physicality, especially when it's taught in a controlled environment, can help anyone, especially kids. It's what's missing in a lot of our lives today, especially those part of the Xbox generation.

The human body wasn't designed to sit and stare at a screen all day. We were built as hunters and gatherers and it's important to have some physicality. Its effects on my life alone have been dramatic, and it started me on a path I never would have thought I'd end up on.

# 5

## BREAKING OUT

With my newfound confidence and determination to take control, I started to think about how I could get more freedom. In my spare time I was running wild, fighting all weekend and getting into all sorts of trouble, but I desperately longed for more independence at home and during school hours.

School was the thing we hated most. St Edmund's felt to us like a prison camp. We were becoming obsessed by the girls at our sister school, St Clare's College, but we couldn't see them during the day. The rules were so oppressive, we couldn't handle it any more. I started talking to Dalla about how we could get out. It was impossible to wag school. One day Dalla and I tried, persuading one of his older brothers' girlfriends to call the school to say we were sick. Unfortunately, she made just the one call, saying we were both sick. Obviously, that was immediately suspicious and, as well, the school secretary knew my mum from working in the tuckshop and would have recognised her voice. We were both busted.

I talked to Mum and Dad about transferring, since my grades were steadily slipping and Year 12 was rapidly approaching. They agreed; I think they were pleased I might be taking an interest in my education. So Dalla, Matt and a few others left St Edmund's at the end of Year 10 and enrolled at the public school Narrabundah College to do our final two years. It was a co-ed government-run college for year 11 and 12 students and had a reputation for having a far more relaxed approach to schooling.

At first that freedom felt great. We were allowed to smoke in the quadrangle, we called teachers by their first names and we could choose either to attend classes, or not. I was with all my closest friends, and we had a great time together. We basically did whatever we wanted. We skipped classes, smoked dope up the back of the school and did the bare minimum to get by. For an extra credit you could work on the radio station that pumped through the school, and I immediately signed on.

I'd always loved music and I was getting into the local hip-hop scene. In particular I adored rap music. NWA was a favourite group and their song 'Fuck the Police' was my favourite song, especially when I was mad with Dad, or he was mad with me. At those times I'd go to my room and take great delight in playing it at full volume, along with WC and the Maad Circle's 'Fuck My Daddy'. When it was Mum I was angry with, it'd be Body Count's 'Momma's Gotta Die Tonight'.

I guess I did go a bit over the top, but my life was one heady mix of desires, hormones and new emotions and, having none of the skills to deal with this, it was getting messy. The only time I seemed to be happy was when I was with my friends, and all my family could do was watch me become more and more distant.

## Pat de Gelder, mum

You tend to bring up your children how you were brought up yourself, and I was brought up quite strictly. Steve was too. As a result we had strict rules in the house, things like eating your dinner at the table, no eating in front of the TV and you'd get whacked if your elbows were on the table. As well I've always been a neat freak, and I like things to be neat and tidy. That was hard with a big family and Steve away so much. We were also very poor in those days. I used to go to the clothing pool for the kids' clothes and I used to cut their hair – until Paul started shaving his head.

To me Paul was always my reliable child, a good boy. Maybe I expected more out of him than he probably thought he should give. He's never liked being told what to do, which is why he didn't like St Edmund's particularly. He was always close to his mates and went around in a group of friends. I didn't know anything about the stuff he got up to outside the house until he told me about it later. I sat with my mouth open when I heard. I knew he wasn't going so well at school but I didn't know how much trouble he was getting into. I thought it was normal high spirits, and I was too busy with everything else going on to take much notice.

Dalla and I, left to our own devices, would rap together constantly. We'd sit around, put on an instrumental track, then I'd write rhymes for hours at a time. We'd practise them at home then, when we go to clubs on the weekends, sometimes we'd ask the DJs to put on our instrumental so we could rap for the crowd. Most of the time they'd tell us to piss off, but a couple of times they let us and we nervously put on a bit of a show. We loved it.

We also did a lot of dancing. Dalla would choreograph a whole routine for our mates and at one stage we practised every day at lunchtime and then for four hours after school each day. Dalla was really good at pulling off all the moves, and we'd do our best to copy him. We went along and performed at Canberra's Youth Dance Festival for kids from high schools and colleges across the region – like the Rock Eisteddfod – and did so well they asked us to come back the next year, even though we'd be finished school by then.

The rap fed into our other classes too. In Spanish, which I loved, as I'd always had a bit of a thing for languages, I'd go in from listening to rap songs in Spanish to asking the teacher what all the rude lyrics meant. But as for the rest of the subjects, like maths, economics and biology, I just wasn't interested. I remember sitting one biology exam stoned out of my brain. I got 36 per cent and my teacher called Mum in for an interview. I couldn't explain why I did so badly; I wasn't going to tell her the real reason.

Weed was absolutely everywhere, and a lot of people I knew smoked it as a social thing. If we weren't having a cone or joint at school, we'd be doing it up the hill from the bus stop, smoking an old grandfather's pipe, busting our lungs. We'd come away totally ripped and have to make our way unsteadily down that hill to catch the bus – one time on all fours. On weekends we'd go to the causeway or to the other side of Lake Burley Griffin, where there are hundreds of rabbits running around. Stoned, we'd drive down in a car and try to run them down – but were so out of it we never managed a single one. Sometimes a group of guys would sit on the bonnet of a car with golf clubs, trying to hit the rabbits. They were never successful either.

Canberra is the kind of place you do things like that. It was so dead boring you had to try to make your own dumb entertainment.

### Travis de Gelder, younger brother

Paul always had a lot of friends and they were more family to him than his real family. Once he'd established his friendship networks, he drifted away from the family.

From around the age of 16 there was a lot of friction at home. He could sometimes be pig-headed. He was in a fair bit of trouble and at times seemed to have an appetite for it. But he was rarely caught; he was smart. He and his friends would watch each other's backs.

### Sean de Gelder, youngest brother

Because I was three years younger than Paul, I never really got to hang out with him. I wanted to, and I looked up to him, but he never wanted to hang out with his younger brothers. He preferred to be with his friends more than his family. I never knew most of the stuff he got up to. He used to hide it pretty well.

But although I was having a lot of fun, I knew I was going nowhere at Narrabundah. My grades had started falling even further from Bs and Cs to Ds, Es and even Fs. The ACT Scaling Test (AST) for all Year 12 students in Canberra, the equivalent to the HSC, was coming up and I felt I didn't have a hope in hell of scoring well. Some of my other friends were studying hard, had jobs in their spare time and were driving cars they'd bought themselves. By contrast I wasn't going forward at all with my life, just smoking weed, drinking, fighting and stealing things. So Dalla, Matt and I got together and started talking it over, and decided we'd probably be better off back at St Edmund's.

I took a deep breath and went to Mum and Dad, telling them I wanted to go back. They took a lot of convincing. After all, I'd been so determined to leave St Edmund's and go to Narrabundah, so sure that it was the right thing for me, and now here I was asking to switch back again. To them it must have seemed that I was just causing trouble. But it wasn't intentional. I truly realised I wasn't going anywhere at that school. Eventually they agreed to let me switch back and, kitted out once again in the St Edmund's uniform, Dalla and I turned up for our big first day.

Typically, we were late and at morning assembly we were glared at every time we whispered a comment to each other. Afterwards, we were taken to a classroom by our form master and ordered to take off our earrings and the rings on our fingers. We were then given a good talking-to: *This is what we expect of you, this is what you can't do, and this is what you have to do.* I snuck a look at Dalla. He was shaking his head. We had two classes before lunchtime and then got together in the break and talked it over. The discipline was even worse than we'd remembered. I guess even though we weren't motivated enough to do well at Narrabundah, this felt as though it would crush the life out of us. We decided we just couldn't take it after all.

So as the bell sounded for lunch, we grabbed our bags from our lockers. A couple of our classmates asked us what we were doing. 'We're out of here!' we told them. And the next minute, we were. We raced back to Narrabundah College and hung out with our mates in the quad in our St Edmund's uniforms while we decided how the hell we were going to break the news of what we'd done to our parents.

When I told mine, predictably, they weren't too pleased. They'd spent a lot of time and energy getting us back into St Edmund's – and here I was throwing it back in their faces. They were under a lot of financial pressure at the time and, with the school fees they'd had to pay again, that episode had cost them a heap. They were also under a lot of emotional strain. My brother Sean had started getting into trouble – basically following in my footsteps, but not being clever enough to get away with it. I was proving the worst possible role model for my little brothers and sister in not buckling down at school, working hard and getting good grades. My dad was probably very disappointed in me. While he had no idea of the extent of the trouble I got into, I'm sure he couldn't have been so high up in the police force and *not* know some of it. It sure as hell wasn't a good look for a police officer's son. Both him and my mum were at their wits' end, and seemed to be arguing more than usual, and then yelling at us even more. I think they were both frustrated that I'd just come

43

and go from home as I liked, contribute nothing and seemed to be going nowhere fast.

I guess at that age you just really want to be left alone to live your life, and when you get a bit lost or go down the wrong track, your parents get upset and start pushing you and pushing you until you feel alienated, and act even worse. That's what happened to me, and it was happening with Sean too. It's not parents' fault; they're doing it because they care. But they don't understand. To a certain extent I think parents have to let their kids just *be* a bit more. They need to be there for them, show love and care, and hang on for the ride, hoping for the best, helping out where they can, and wait for them finally to see sense.

The morning after we'd turfed St Edmund's I returned to Narrabundah, swearing I'd do better. But I didn't. I just went back to hanging out with my mates and often I wouldn't even go home at night. I'd stay at the place of two friends, Indonesian girls who had a nice apartment in Kingston, whose parents were paying for them to study in Canberra. My parents were always worrying, nagging me to be home early and go to school and try harder. I wouldn't listen and they got more and more angry. And when the exams came round, I walked out halfway through. My parents were beside themselves.

On the last day of Year 12 my dad called me on the phone at the Indonesian girls' flat. I was wary. He had something he wanted to tell me, he said.

'Yeah, what's that?' I asked. He was blunt. It was to come home, collect my shit and then go. I wasn't welcome any more.

I hung up in shock and thought, *Whoa! Where the hell am I*

*going to go? What the hell am I going to do?* Suddenly, I had no home, no qualifications and absolutely no prospects.

Finally, I had the absolute freedom I'd always craved. It didn't feel anything like I'd imagined. For the first time in my life I was completely on my own.

# A WASTE OF SPACE

While I was scared about being on my own, I told myself to look on the positive side. This could be a good thing, an opportunity to reinvent myself. But in the meantime I applied myself simply to pissing my prospects up the wall – doing more of what had got me into such a mess in the first place.

The two Indonesian girls – bless them – agreed to take me in. They were amazingly kind to me, especially since I was fast turning into a waste of space. I signed on to the dole to get a cheque each fortnight and then slept in, got up late, ate the girls' leftover sambal or rice and vegies or whatever they'd cooked, and mooched around the rest of the time. I did pretty much nothing at all but smoke a pack of cigarettes a day, and plenty of weed. I'd sit around hanging out for the weekend when I'd blow the rest of my money on some drinks with my friends, smoking cones and having a good time.

To earn extra money I started selling drugs, just on a small scale and only ever weed. I bought the first ounce for $240, scraped together from my dole money and income from shoplifting, then broke it into sticks, measuring it out carefully: a quarter of an ounce would be 18 grams, and one stick would weigh 1 gram. Each stick would sell for $25, or $20 to good customers or my friends. It was such a profitable business it immediately became self-financing. I'd buy it mostly from people I knew, and sell it to other people I knew. Together with the dole, it certainly helped me make ends meet. It could occasionally get tricky, though. One friend started complaining to me about his girlfriend smoking too much weed, and I'd think, *But she's my best customer!* I sympathised with him and felt bad, but kept on secretly supplying her. On her own she provided me with $75 a week.

I was smoking a chunk of my profits, and the much weed was taking a huge toll on my mind. I was getting more and more paranoid, some days getting too scared to even leave the house. So eventually I cut it out altogether. The dealing was getting more problematic too. It all started feeling much dodgier when strangers began rocking up on the doorstep in the middle of the night, asking to score.

As well as the drugs and the drink, the fighting continued uninterrupted. Violence just seemed to follow me and my mates around. Even when we tried not to get into any trouble, we did. There was one evening when we all made a pact not to fight; we'd just go out for a few drinks and some fun. But before the night was up, someone put a shoulder into a group of guys outside a nightclub and started a fight. Unfortunately, those guys turned out to be friends with the security guards and we copped a flogging. On the walk home afterwards we were all arguing among ourselves. *Couldn't we just for once go out without having a fight?* It started getting heated, and we began pushing each other around in a car park, then before we knew it, we were all fighting again – this time with each other.

I think that was it for us. We knew the fighting was getting out of hand when there wasn't a single evening we couldn't *not* fight. I was also nervous about getting a criminal record. I'd had a few close calls with the police and one night when I was out and had had a huge argument with a good friend, I kicked a bus shelter window and shattered it. As I was walking off I saw some cops coming towards me. I ducked into a bar and sidled up to a Rastafarian dude I knew and told him that if they came in to say I'd been there all night. But they didn't even look at him. They came in and just dragged me outside. I got taken to court over that and realised that you only get so many chances before you get thrown into the big house. I knew at least one guy who'd been in and out of juvenile detention pretty much all his life, and I sure as hell didn't want to end up like him.

Looking back, it was a terrible way to live. It was such a waste. Life's about exploring and developing who you are and I was doing exactly the opposite. Doing drugs steals your brain, your thoughts, your memories, your time. Selling them is even worse. The first couple of times I felt bad, but if you do it enough, you learn to cope. It's stupid and it doesn't make it better, but it does make it easier. Like my customers, I got nothing out of it at all. I ended up unhealthy, skinny, eating only junk food, and was out of my brain half the time with booze and weed. That's all time that I'll never get back.

A lot of what happens to you depends on what, and who, you surround yourself with. It's easy to become a drug addict if you hang out with drug addicts. It makes it simpler to rationalise it, to give it a go, but before you know it you're scratching your skin off and living in a ditch. I had friends who got into drugs big time, and ended up dead or in prison or went into drug-induced psychoses, and turned out quite different to how they used to be. It wasn't nice at all.

I guess all the drinking, drugs and fighting were rites of passage. Back then I did some crazy stuff drunk or wasted on drugs. I just felt lucky, at times, to come out of it alive. But sometimes I'd think I'd have to pay for it later in life.

Finally, to try and break the cycle, my friend Brock got me a job as a kitchen hand in a restaurant in Manuka where he was an apprentice chef. I washed his dishes and helped cook the tapas menu. It started opening my eyes to what was possible. I was working for money for the first time, and it was so much more rewarding than bludging off the government. We worked hard there, with crap pay, and I lost count of the times I cut or burnt myself, but finally I was actually legitimately earning some cash.

After a while, I moved out of the girls' flat, and four of us from the restaurant moved into a house in Deakin together. But life still felt so difficult, and so aimless. I hadn't talked to my parents since Dad kicked me out, and I wasn't having much to do with my brothers and sister either. I'd cut myself off from them.

## Steve de Gelder

I'd just come home from working in Brisbane, walked in late and Travis and Sean had been fighting in the bedroom. Pat said something about it being hard to manage with the boys fighting and Paul being no help as she didn't know where he was. So I rang him and told him to get his stuff and get out. It was spur-of-the-moment stuff, and Paul did go. I'd told the kids all many times that if they didn't like the rules, they could go, but this time Paul actually went. I didn't really mean it, but Paul took it literally, and did. Of course I felt bad.

I was 20 and had absolutely nothing to show for it. I was just a stealing, durry-punching, goon-bag-drinking, drug-pushing, bong-smoking kid, now working in a kitchen as the lowest of the low. When I started looking at myself and my life so far, I realised the hole I was in. I had no prospects and nothing to offer. After 11 years in Canberra, I'd come to hate it, and I was bored just getting stoned and drunk with my friends.

My mate Matt had gone to live in Brisbane, and I called him up and had a chat. He said there was a spare room going where he was living and he might be able to get me a job behind the bar at the place where he worked. I wasn't sure.

That weekend I got into a really big fight and ended up surrounded by 20 guys. I was saved when an older mate arrived and pulled me out of the melee, bloody and bruised, but it felt like the very last straw. I was sick of the place, of fighting all the time with other drunk and bored people. I was fed up with selling weed and smoking it myself. I desperately needed a change of scenery. I wanted excitement, and I longed for adventure.

So I bought an old car from Brock's parents – they weren't to know I didn't have a licence and had never been taught to drive properly – and threw in all my possessions in the world, which didn't add up to much. I then turned the key in the ignition and just drove off, out of my life and everything I knew.

# 7.

## SEX 'N' DRUGS AND RAP 'N' SOUL

The music was pounding in my chest, there were disco lights flashing everywhere and the woman in front of me was slowly peeling off her shirt. She was undoing the buttons one at a time, her breasts straining against the flimsy silk. She finally pulled it apart and flung it to the ground, before moving her hips in a slow grind against the pole between her legs.

I felt a slight sweat on my top lip as she began stroking the top of her stockinged legs and wriggling her tight little skirt above her panties. It was every man's dream come true . . .

A voice broke my reverie.

'Oi, barman!' it called. 'BARMAN! I need a drink over here!' Reluctantly, I tore my eyes away, just as the woman on stage was doing the same with that skirt.

'Yes, sir,' I said sharply. 'Same again?'

It had been two weeks since I'd set off from Canberra to start a new life, and so far it seemed to be turning out rather nicely. I'd been worrying all the way on that long drive up to Brisbane about how things might work out, and had played my hip-hop music tapes loud on the stereo to try to block my anxiety. Not having a driver's licence, I wasn't helped either by seeing police cars going the other way and having a few sit behind me for a while. Every time I noticed them, my stomach would do a backflip and I'd get nervous. Just one wrong move and my adventure would take a whole new turn.

I'd had a break on the way, visiting Brock at Port Macquarie, where he'd moved from Canberra a few months earlier, then headed off back up the Pacific Highway. I pulled up at the first service station I hit coming into Brisbane and called Matt. He said he'd come and meet me. It was 8 p.m. on 23 March 1998. My 21st birthday.

We stopped to buy a carton of beer and then went to his place. He was living with two other guys at the time in a rented house they'd christened 'The Pink Palace'. The walls were all painted pink, and out in the front yard there were sprayed pink car tyres cut into the shape of flamingos. The housemates were both working at record shops during the day and Matt worked as a DJ in a club – a strip club – and was sure he'd be able to get me a job behind the bar. I said I couldn't think of anything I'd like to do more.

The club was big and pretty fancy, with pole dancing, stripping, a glass-walled shower and a big foamy spa bath in the centre of the stage, with fantasy rooms out back. Hen's nights, when the guys stripped for the girls, could be terrifying. I can honestly tell you that there is nothing more frightening than 150 drunk and horny women with easy access to a naked man. One night I was on my break, helping clear tables, when all the women thought it'd be a great idea if I got up on stage and gave them an impromptu show. They started chanting my name and grabbing at my clothes. One woman even stuck a fiver in my pants before screaming like a banshee and trying to get at my belt. I was out of there so quickly. I could still hear them chanting from downstairs.

But generally it was a fun place to work. The girls were mostly lovely and really friendly with the two bar staff, as we kept an eye on them as well as serving the drinks. I was a bit of a favourite, I think, because I was so young and probably quite innocent. I'd often give them free drinks when there weren't many customers in. I was still a skinny kid with a shaved head and the girls sort of looked out for me too.

I became good friends with some of them, including one girl called Riley, who was a former *Penthouse* Pet of the Month. In the quiet times we'd play pool together. Sometimes she'd lean over and the sight of her tits would put me off my shot. I never complained.

It was a whole new way of life, and I embraced it wholeheart-edly. Suddenly my best friends were Matt and a whole bunch of hot strippers. One had sold me her old motorbike and I loved that too. The starter motor was broken so it had to be jump-started each time. I had to figure out how to ride it myself, just like I'd done with learning to drive, and imagined starting it would be similar. I put it in gear and pointed it downhill, easing back the clutch and pumping the throttle. So, again with no licence, and only dressed in shorts and a T-shirt with no helmet and – luckily – not much gravel rash, one of the greatest love affairs of my life began.

There were a couple of gangsters who were regulars at the bar, Rocket and Snap, and they always came in with their guns, and were pretty intimidating to a young fella like me. They always got free scotch and Jack Daniels . . . just in case. Snap, who seemed to be in charge, was dating one of the bar girls and he invited a couple of us to his place for a party once. I ended up having a half-hour conversation with a hitman, who was celebrating his retirement. I was quizzing him about his life and my friend standing next to me kept elbowing me and hissing, 'Paul, SHUT UP! He *kills* people for a living!' I got pretty friendly with his girlfriend at one point too, but she chickened out of actually consummating our relationship. In retrospect, thank God. If her boyfriend had found out, I'm not sure either of us would have been around for a second round.

There was plenty of sex elsewhere, in any case. One evening the manager and I closed up early, picked up two girls at a club and took them back to our club. We soaped up the girls in the tub and had sex there, then against the stripper poles and again on a lambskin rug we flung on the pool table. We ended up having sex almost everywhere in that club.

In my free time I'd started playing with music again, writing rhymes and gathering instrumentals. I was listening to music constantly, not only rap but also rhythm and blues, and soul, with Curtis Mayfield and Nina Simone particular favourites. The club next to ours, Euphoria, played R&B and hip-hop, and I'd often go in for a drink and a listen. Matt was starting to get a bit of a name for himself as a DJ too, and one of our flatmates was heavily into the Brisbane hip-hop world. He and some of his friends ran a Sunday-night gig at Euphoria and had a weekly hip-hop show on community radio. I hung out with them one night at the club, and seeing as everyone else was dropping rhymes, I did a bit of a rap too and they seemed very surprised and a little impressed.

I ended up doing some work with my flatmate on his show, mostly answering the phones and chatting up the girls, and I started hanging out with him and his crew. There were 11 of us in total, and I was the only Aussie white boy – the rest were from all over the place: Sri Lanka, the Philippines, Malaysia, the Cook Islands and the US. We needed more space to work together and eventually five of us moved into a huge two-storey, five-bedroom apartment in Fortitude Valley.

Every day we'd get together to make music, drink and play pool, and muck around with the DJ and production gear. With a lot of work from the flatmate in charge, we got a Friday-night spot hosting a hip-hop party called 'Da Joint' at The Gig nightclub, and running hip-hop nights occasionally on a Saturday. Before long we'd built up a bit of a reputation, and even recorded an EP, called *The Sixth Sense*. I jumped on my mate Kris's track 'Smokin' Hydro', and did the first two verses, while he did the third and sung the hook. It ended up being picked up by Triple J on the Australian music show and was played for five weeks straight.

It was great to have that exposure and to be able to play our own tracks on our radio show and at the club, but we needed a way to showcase the crew and do a big show. Our chance came when we scored the supporting gig for the biggest rapper of the day, US star Snoop Dogg. It was his first visit to Australia and his tour was a complete sell-out nationally. His album *Doggystyle* was the first debut album ever to hit the Billboard charts at number one, and with his gangster background he was the ultimate rap celebrity. The week before we were due to play, we received a call from the touring company bringing Snoop out to Australia.

'We asked you to play for half an hour,' they said. 'But do you think you could make it an hour and a half instead?' Everyone was pumped. *An hour and a half!*

For the opening of our set we performed 'Smokin' Hydro', and a friend who made props for Movie World constructed a huge mock stereo system and a massive six-foot joint that lit up and blew smoke out the end, courtesy of a few smoke machines. At the start of the gig the stage was engulfed in the smoke from the joint and then Kris and I walked out of it to sing our song in front of 3000 people. It was incredible, one of the most amazing moments of my life. The crowd went wild, and the US basketball import Andre Moore, who was playing for the Brisbane Bullets, shouted to Matt, who was sitting next to him, 'Snoop will have to be bloody good to compete with *that!*' It was a real adrenalin-pumping experience.

After my song I spent the rest of our time on stage bouncing around the set, drinking and kicking soccer balls we'd been given by the Brisbane Strikers out into the crowd. Burkes Brewing Company, which makes a beer filtered through hemp, marijuana's non-psychoactive cousin, had given us a carton, so we drank that up on stage too. It was all such a great buzz.

We held the official afterparty at The Gig and, with some of Snoop's crew, rocked on into the night. DJ Jam did a set on the turntables and we all wandered in and out of the VIP room, dancing with the girls and drinking. One of Snoop's crew challenged me to a joint-rolling competition. I rolled a 16-paper joint that looked more like a humungous white cigar and won hands down.

For a time I thought that this was it: I was on my way to a music career. We pooled all our money and threw a big party to raise enough cash to have 1000 copies of the EP pressed. We used them mostly for promotions, trying to get a deal with a record company. It was a hard slog, but it felt like this was what I was meant to be doing with my life.

At this point I got back in contact with my family too. Although Dad had kicked me out, I was never really pissed off with him. I knew I'd been a pain to live with and him doing what he did, I now realised, was a good thing. It had made me go out in the world and do things for myself rather than staying at home and being a drain on him and Mum. Even though a couple of years had passed since we'd been in contact, I was proud of what I was doing in the music industry and I wanted to share it with my family. I wanted them to know that, no matter what had happened in the past, I was okay. I was doing well, having loads of fun with my mates, the girls and all the musos and, professionally, teetering on the brink of my biggest break yet. They were happy I seemed to be actually doing something with my life although, secretly, I'm sure they thought, *Here we go again; this won't work out either*.

But as the days stretched into weeks, and the weeks into months, I discovered that a music career isn't just about talent and wanting something enough. I'd say it's 5 per cent talent, 20 per cent determination and 75 per cent luck – being in the right place at the right time with the right bunch of people who have the right contacts. Try as we might, we just couldn't get signed.

By this time I was only doing a couple of shifts a week at the strip club, and spending the rest of my time on the music. To try to push things along we even enrolled in the government's New Enterprise Incentive Scheme (NEIS) to learn how to write a business plan so we could apply for funds to get us off the ground. But by the end of the course I still had no idea what I was doing. Learning about business plans, doing the figures and having to write documents for government approval felt far beyond the scope of what I wanted to do. I was just interested in being a rapper and partying and having groupies.

Even worse, because I'd had to quit the club to have time for the classes, I had much less money – the NEIS payments were even less than the dole. The rows between the band and the flat-mate in charge, who'd been smoking more and more weed and getting steadily more aggressive, were getting worse and worse, and everyone's patience was wearing as thin as our cash reserves. Life was becoming more of a struggle every day. Eventually, after a year and a half, the whole thing fell apart. I quit, and a few of the others followed.

### Matt Nugent, friend

When I first met Paul at school, he was quite reserved, not terribly outgoing and a bit lost somehow. As he grew older, I think all the fighting and stuff was a way of compensating for that, a way of impressing people. He didn't have much confidence, and it was almost as if he was seeking other people's approval.

His real passions were skateboarding, martial arts and then music but, by the time he left school, he'd never really worked out what he wanted to do; he was confused. But he was also very headstrong and would only do what he wanted to do. When he did the support for Snoop Dogg in Brisbane, he really commanded the stage. But when everything there fell apart, he was lost again.

A friend and I moved into another house, surviving on our $300-a-fortnight dole payments – just enough to cover the rent with a tiny amount left over for food. My fortunes plummeted from some of the greatest moments of my life to some of the bleakest. It was a terrible house, with no electricity, no hot water, no beds and not even any cutlery. Our couch was a boxing bag. We'd had a tiny battery-run TV donated to us, and in order to watch it we had to keep a finger on the 'on' button at all times. The faint glow from the screen was our only light at night. Friends donated plastic knives and forks and gave us hot water for our staple fare: two-minute noodles. We only managed to shower every day by sneaking down to the public swimming area at nearby South Bank.

We tried to make the best of a bad job, but it was hard. The walls between the rooms were so thin my mate in the next room recorded me having sex and then played it back to friends, clear as a bell.

I managed to get work in a couple of restaurants and, in one, was offered a promotion to bar manager. I was pleased. After so many false starts I thought maybe this was my way forward in the world. Then I took a long hard look at the guy I was meant to be replacing. He was a tall, skinny, pale bloke, sucking constantly on a durry, looking worried and going home to his wife in the suburbs every evening at the end of the shift. Nice enough bloke, but I thought, *Do I really want to be that guy?*

As soon as I'd asked myself the question, I knew the answer. I'd hit another dead end.

All those hot naked chicks and the pumping rap scene had been a pretty exciting interlude, but they hadn't led me anywhere. For a while I thought I'd found my true vocation with music, until that all fell to pieces. Now I was back living week to week, never having enough money to do anything much, and still having nothing to show for myself. I was 23, I had no qualifications to talk of, I had little contact with my family and I seemed to have taken one step forward, and two steps back.

I felt sure there was something bigger in life waiting for me, but I had no idea what it might be or how to find out what it was. Yet somehow I knew I'd have to work out what I wanted to do.

So far I'd just been floating along, jumping on any life raft that happened to drift into view and going along for the ride. Often that had turned out to be great fun, taking me in amazing directions – like the strip club – that I'd otherwise never have thought of. But once the novelty had worn off, each time I'd found myself in a dead-end job with not much money and few prospects. When I'd tried to do different things, like with the band, everything had turned to shit. Maybe I had a defeatist attitude and dropped things as soon as they got too hard – or maybe I realised when things weren't right, and was prepared to move on to something new. But I certainly knew that it was proving harder to keep my head above water, and the struggle was beginning to wear me down.

I felt now that I really needed a purpose, a focus, an aim, something I could get excited about and that would challenge me. My friends were all starting to sort themselves out. Matt was getting a real name for himself DJing, and he loved it. In Canberra Dalla was going back to college and studying physiology to become a personal trainer and do remedial massage. Brock was well on the way to becoming a chef. Another friend, who loved drawing, had found a great job with a company producing comics. If I wasn't careful, I'd be completely left behind as the sad, broke friend who turned up to sleep on their sofas every so often.

I knew I'd have to do something drastic to get out of the rut. And so, finally, I did.

# PART TWO

# ADAPT

# 8

## SIGNING MY LIFE AWAY

He was friendly, he was jovial and he assured us we'd made a great decision. All the way there we chilled out, chatting, laughing, making new friends and generally getting to know each other. But when the bus finally pulled up at Kapooka, near Wagga Wagga in New South Wales, the home of the defence department's Blamey Barracks, suddenly everything changed.

His voice went up to about 180 decibels and he started screaming at us.

'GET OFF THE FUCKING BUS!' he yelled. 'NOW! HURRY UP! GET OFF, GET OFF!' It just about made us shit our pants. We all stared at him in shock, then scurried to do as he'd ordered. It was our very first experience as the newest recruits of the Australian Army, and the first of many times to come when I'd ask myself what the fuck I was doing there.

He lined us up on the concrete in front of the bus and took a good look at us. I could feel myself shrinking under his gaze. Although I was older than some of the others, he made me feel as small as I had back on my first day at my very first school. He demanded we hand over our phones and any knives, and he stashed them all in bags. Then he not so much marched us, since we didn't know yet how to march, as herded us briskly down to the accommodation blocks at the barracks. There, we were handed our army camouflage uniforms and Physical Training (PT) gear. Our civvies were whisked away and, from that point on, our lives became a living hell.

Joining the army had seemed like quite a good idea. After hitting a brick wall in Brisbane, I'd decided, yet again, to try to change my circumstances, to give myself a fresh start. Both my brothers had joined the army and I wondered how they were liking it. I was by that stage calling home every now and again, so I spoke to Mum about how everyone was going and mentioned my idea about joining the army. If she was surprised, she didn't show it. She told me how much Sean and Travis were enjoying their army careers and said, yes, she thought I should give it a go. When I talked it over with my mate Dalla, he was just as encouraging. 'I think it sounds like a great idea,' he told me.

My youngest brother, Sean, had joined the army first, straight from the Army Reserve in Year 12. He'd immediately got a trip overseas, to East Timor, and had seen some action over there, which sounded great. He was the one who'd taken all my bad traits and really run with them. While I'd got away with most things, he ended up getting caught much more often, but signing up for the army, and being subjected to its discipline, had really helped put him back on track.

My other brother, Travis, who was a lot quieter, had followed Sean into the artillery division and was loving it too. He was football-oriented like Sean and liked the idea of playing sport, hanging out with the boys and drinking beer. I called him and said I was thinking of joining. He was shocked. He said I was the last person he thought would ever sign up. With all the weed and music and bars and the kind of people I'd been hanging out with, my life was a total contrast to how it would be as part of the forces. He said he wasn't sure I'd like someone else having authority over me and, because I'd always been so independent – or pig-headed, as he put it – he didn't know if I'd be able to cope. Sean felt much the same. Since I could never usually get up before 10 a.m., he wondered if I'd ever manage 5.30 a.m.

I thought about that a lot, but the more I looked back on my life and dwelled on what it would be like if I just continued along the same path, the more it seemed that the army might be a way forward. I'd be receiving a regular wage, I'd be learning new things and I'd get to work out and drink beer with mates, all of which had their own attractions. And, of course, I did have the hair for it. After shaving my head at 16, I'd found it so easy I'd kept it like that ever since.

I went along to the defence forces' recruitment office and had a look through all the brochures. They were full of cool-sounding jobs like 'assault pioneer', which sounded like it was from *Star Wars* – exciting, challenging and full of the promise of blowing things up and shooting at things. For some reason that appealed to me enormously. I wanted to carry a big gun, shoot rockets, jump out of planes and go riding in helicopters. It seemed I really wanted to be a soldier.

The main hurdle to getting in, I knew, would be my past drug use. I'd finished with drugs and that part of my life was over, but how could I convince the defence forces of that? I was desperate to start afresh. Now, there's a system in place that offers counselling if you admit to involvement with drugs, with the chance then to reapply. In any case, I'm grateful to the forces for giving me a second chance at life. The fitness test was pretty easy – running between witches' hats and then doing sit-ups and push-ups – all that kickboxing training I'd done in the past really helped. I found the aptitude test simple too.

Finally came the psychological evaluation. It's one of my most vivid memories: the psych doing the whole good cop–bad cop routine, trying to see how I'd react under scrutiny and pressure. It was a very confusing experience but, as I left his office, he smiled and said, 'Good luck with your career!' That stopped me in my tracks. I thought, *My God! I've finally got a career!* Having gone from job to job, I felt like that was such a bizarre concept. But having something that I could build on and grow and develop – I liked the thought of it. Suddenly, it felt like I'd already accomplished something.

But I still had one more decision to make. My brothers had both been adamant about which branch of the army I should choose to go into: the artillery, like them. But whatever I decided, they said, one thing was for sure. I should avoid the infantry like the plague. Of course, I couldn't have my little brothers tell me what to do and immediately went for the infantry. If I was going into battle, I wanted to be right up in the front line, not in the cheap seats at the back, away from all the action.

On the day in November 2000 when I caught that bus to the barracks, six weeks after I'd first applied to join, I remember thinking how sad it was that I could pack all my stuff into two suitcases. I no longer had a car – earlier I'd crashed it after driving drunk and stoned, sliding it sideways into the gutter so both the wheels on one side had folded under it, leaving it a worthless wreck. I'd had to sell my bike as it was getting old and I had no money to fix it. As I picked up those two cases I felt that my life as I'd known it, with all the drugs and struggles and working in clubs, was over. That was all I knew, and for many years I'd been running my own routine. Now I was going to be surrounded by new people and be given a uniform and a regiment and orders, and I was going to be at the bottom of the barrel. I felt a bit scared.

Kapooka, where all the new recruits do their 80-day training course, didn't look a terribly inviting place. We were bundled four to a room, with a six-foot-high divider down the middle, two beds either side. By the foot of each bed was a locker. Everything in there had to be neatly folded and in a very precise position, we were told, and the beds had to be stripped and remade with hospital corners every morning. Lights-out was at 10 p.m. By then it was pretty close to that time, so we all went to bed. I lay there for a while, wondering what I'd got myself into, and what life would be like as a member of 12 Platoon, The Purple Devils, before finally falling into a deep sleep.

I woke with a start to the loud crack of machine-gun fire very,

very close. I stayed frozen where I was, wondering what the fuck was going on. It turned out we were being given our first morning reveille courtesy of blanks being fired down the hallway. The noise suddenly stopped and the Redgum song 'I was Only 19', about the Vietnam War, burst out over the loudspeakers. We all lay there, listening to the words, really hearing them for the first time. It was an amazing song and it felt strange hearing it as I was going into the next phase of my life with the army.

But the lull was soon over.

'GET OUT OF BED! GET OUT OF BED!' came the yell from the corridor. 'HURRY UP! *NOW!*' We all leapt to our feet, tore the sheets off our beds, flung them over our shoulders and raced out to the hallway for morning inspection. We'd already been warned that this was the army's way; it was part of the drill to make our beds each morning. Apparently in the past some guys had tried to get out of it to snatch a few minutes' extra shut-eye or save time on morning duties by sleeping under their beds – so it'd look as if they'd just made them. Now we had to pull our beds apart each morning before putting them back together again.

As I stood there in the hallway, swaying with tiredness, shivering with cold, and knowing that I'd have just 15 minutes to make the bed, fight for a shower down the corridor, tear half the skin off my face with a razor in the hurry to shave, get dressed and clean the bathrooms before having everything inspected, I had a moment of doubt. I'd been kicked out of home because I couldn't stand the discipline, and then left St Edmund's because I'd found it too oppressive. And now here I was, being shouted at by the most discipline-crazy people I could possibly find.

If I wasn't already insane, what on earth would I be like by the time my new-recruit training was up? Not to mention, of course, the four years I'd signed up for. With every minute, it was beginning to look more and more like a lifetime.

# 9

## DOES A SOLDIER SHIT IN THE WOODS?

I'd expected the regime to be tough at Kapooka. We had a lot to
learn as new recruits – physical training, parade drill, first aid,
basic military and weapons combat training, night-fighting, navigation, field-craft . . . But it would come as no surprise to anyone
who knew me that what I really struggled with was the discipline,
the complete and utter micro-managing of almost every moment
of my life. I'd found it hard at home with Mum and Dad and even
harder at St Edmund's, but I'd taken a deep breath and jumped
right in with the army, hoping I'd be able to cope. After all, I'd
had so much freedom in the last few years and that hadn't really
worked out for me, so surely now, I told myself, I was a bit more
mature and would be able to manage being ordered around. But it
was far tougher than I'd imagined. We were barked at constantly
and had someone watching us every minute of the day, telling us

exactly what we could do. They said 'Jump' and we didn't even ask how high. We just started jumping and hoped to hell it was high enough.

After the first couple of days I started to realise how hard we were going to be working. At 10 p.m. every night it was lights out and no talking. We didn't have the energy to bitch about it even if we'd wanted to. We just went straight to sleep, absolutely busted from the day. Mind you, if there were any breaks during the day, we did have a moan about it all to our fellow soldiers-in-training. In the army we're all professional whingers.

Unlike school, this time there was no way out. Some people snapped, or just did runners and disappeared, or tried to go for the soft option, saying they were sick or injured when they weren't. But that could be risky. It was classified as 'malingering' and was a chargeable offence. Even getting sunburnt to the point where you couldn't work was considered malingering. People had to be incredibly imaginative, like saying they had a sore back, which couldn't easily be disproved, or diarrhoea, although then you had to take a crap and somehow collect a small portion in a container for testing to make sure you didn't have something seriously wrong. The only other way out was going to the padre and saying you were losing it and thinking of killing yourself or everyone else. That'd get you out. Later, when I went to my battalion, I discovered about one soldier every year actually went through with the threat to commit suicide and would be found hanging from the ceiling fan in their room. But for me, however hard it was, it wasn't an option. I knew it was a new experience and I had to give it time. I didn't want to be a quitter and, besides, I didn't have anything to go back to.

NO TIME FOR FEAR

The infantry is billed by the army as an elite group of soldiers who work in challenging, diverse and sometimes very remote environments, and who have high standards of mental and physical toughness. In retrospect I guess I shouldn't have been surprised the training was so hard. But it did come as a bit of a shock to the system.

Every morning we did PT, lots of running and even more pack marches. We started off slowly, marching 3 kilometres with all our webbing – the system of straps and pouches soldiers use to carry all their battle and survival equipment – as well as our rifles and 10-kilogram packs. Over the weeks we worked up to a 20-kilometre march with 7-kilo webbing, our rifles, machine-guns and 15-kilo packs. Those kind of exercises, especially in summer, would usually break people, especially the women, who went through exactly the same training. One woman I saw started having hallucinations during one march and threw off her pack and started dancing and screaming. But as I got used to pushing myself I started to enjoy the marches more and more. Just as I'd loved kickboxing as a kid, I liked the physical challenge and the feeling of getting fitter, stronger and more determined all the time. It sounds a bit sadistic, but seeing other people really hurting spurs you on and makes you feel like you're not doing too badly. My friends had been important to me all my life and as I built mateships with the other recruits, who were going through the same pain, PT became a lot easier. I began looking forward to it each day. By the end of our training I'd won the 12 Platoon award for PT.

I also liked parts of the weapons training. Some of it was

outside and you'd end up lying on the hard red earth propped on your bare elbows for 40 minutes, cocking and uncocking your rifle over and over again. Those days would finish with you sore and bruised, and suffering the ache of tendonitis. On other days we'd go to the weapon-training simulation system, a 12-lane indoor small-arms training facility using laser and computer-based virtual simulation technology. It's like a million-dollar PlayStation where you learn to shoot, in either day or night conditions, without ever actually firing a bullet. That was fun, and since only eight people could go through at a time, if you weren't doing concurrent training – which the army *loves* – you'd have valuable time out sitting on the grass waiting, chatting with each other.

The mateship that develops in these situations is a great plus. Within the platoon, you're split up into sections, nine to each. Because I was beginning to shine in the physical tests and was proving popular with the other guys, I was assigned as second in charge, 2IC. I became best mates with the guys in my section, united by how hard the staff were on us. We bonded over mealtimes as well, in the rush to get as much food into our bodies in the allotted time as we could. I excelled at that too. Breakfast, lunch and dinner were always highlights of every day, and I could jam in a huge amount of food in a very short time. I'd put everything, main plus dessert, on the plate at the same time and just eat. That's called a 'train smash'.

The food in the mess was good but back then the ration packs we were given for out bush – 'ratpacks' – were pretty awful. We'd bet on who could eat a whole can of this stuff called 'beef and veg Dutch-style'. No one ever could. It looked like dog food with things like thick arteries in it and had a horrible gelatinous coating on the outside. We soon learned to throw away half of our ration packs as soon as we got them and, if we had the chance, to go to the shop on base to buy our own food to supplement them.

Sometimes those ration packs gave me real trouble. They had condensed milk in them, chocolate, M&Ms and all sorts of dairy products and, being lactose-intolerant, they'd set up a terrible chain reaction in my guts. One of the first times we went out bush for a couple of days we weren't allowed to use any white light at night – no torches, no flames, anything like that. One evening after I'd eaten my ratpack my corporal went to a meeting. I really needed to go to the toilet, and started getting a terrible stomach ache. I went off to try to find the shitpit but, stumbling around in the pitch-black, I couldn't find it anywhere. There was no starlight, the clouds were shrouding the moon and, after searching round and round, with the pain getting worse by the minute, I couldn't even find the track we'd made.

Finally, I couldn't stand it any more, and just downed drawers where I stood and squatted, leaving a mess on the ground, a kind of landmine waiting for the next unwary soldier. Then I tried to find my way back but, having absolutely no idea where I was, and still not able to see anything, I only succeeded in getting even more lost. Eventually, I thought, *Fuck it!*, and pulled out my army-issue matches, which are half stick and half flint and blaze like flares, and struck one to try to find out where I was. At exactly that moment my corporal happened to walk back down the hill and saw me in this glare of light when he'd expressly ordered a complete blackout. He tore the shit out of me – what was left of it, anyway – and then I had to explain what had happened.

He listened, then said sternly, 'Okay, but I don't want anyone stepping in it, so go find it and bury it.' I walked away, wondering how the hell I was going to be able to find it again. There was nothing for it but to get down on my hands and knees, and crawl around the dirt, trying to locate it by smell. I did this for about 20 minutes with absolutely no joy until finally, in desperation, I lit another match. Unfortunately, the corporal had been standing a few feet away, watching me the whole time. I got torn apart all over again. In the morning meeting, he told everyone what had happened. Of course they all took the piss out of me. In retrospect I suppose it was pretty funny, but I learned a valuable lesson that day: to know when I'd had enough lactose.

The basics of soldiering seemed to come naturally to me. We were instructed on the rudiments of patrolling: how to walk silently, and how to carry your rifle at different stages. If you were patrolling, you'd hold it in a certain grip; if you were searching, your eyes always followed the exact direction your rifle was pointing; and if you came to a point where someone was in front of you, you'd always dip your weapon. All those little things become big things when you're a soldier out in the field. But I hated doing drill, learning to march out on the parade ground. I wanted to be a soldier with a gun, running around the bush and shooting stuff, not a cocker spaniel or a show pony prancing around, making sure everything was just so.

Digging pits – pits to live in, pits to shit in, pits for fighting from – was also . . . the pits. I came to hate that. They give you a tiny shovel called an 'entrenching tool', which is a pole with a shovel bit folding out from one side and a pick you can fold out from the other, and tell you to dig a hole that's big enough to fit your body into. The bare minimum's about two foot deep. Eventually, you're having to dig pits deep enough to stand up in with wooden struts to keep the structure up and overhead protection of corrugated iron cammed up and concealed – that's six foot deep and fifteen foot long, or four days' non-stop digging. You end up out in the bush for ages, blisters all over your hands and dirt everywhere else. It's hard and scary, but it's exciting at the same time.

It's at that point you realise you've finally gone from what they call in the army 'a scum-sucking civvy' to a dirty, stinking soldier carrying a rifle or machine-gun. It's as if the civilian life has been beaten out of you, and civvies are almost the enemy, to be despised as well as protected.

# 10

## PARACHUTING TO GLORY

When I'd talked to my friends about my potential career change, everyone said they'd known someone who'd joined the army and turned into an arsehole. I swore to my mates that wouldn't happen to me; I promised I wouldn't change. But I did change. By the end of the 80 days' training I was definitely no longer the little weed-smoking punk I'd gone in as. I was a lot more confident. I was fit. And I felt more focused than I'd ever before been.

That's not to say, of course, that the transformation was complete. My passing-out parade at Kapooka was at Christmas time so I was allowed to go to my next of kin's for two weeks afterwards. I'd put down my old childhood and strip-club mate Matt as my next of kin – my friends still felt closer than my family – so I went up to Brisbane and hung out with him. I spent the time getting really drunk most nights and enjoying the brief taste of freedom. But before I knew it the two weeks were up, and I was back on the bus and off to the next stage of my army career: Initial Employment Training (IET) at the School of Infantry in Singleton, in NSW's Hunter Valley.

This was a whole new bag of chips. I was used to the discipline by this time, but now I was learning how to be a proper soldier, and being groomed for the specific job I'd be doing in the infantry, which I'd find out about later. It was 11 weeks of men teaching men how to be soldiers, and it was much harder than at Kapooka. For a start, the PT was a lot more demanding, with obstacle courses, weights circuits, and strength and endurance training. The pack marches were longer, carrying more weight. The bush time was tougher. Singleton in January, February and March was a lot hotter than it had been at Kapooka. And it was all so much more hardcore.

On one phase of the course, for instance, they taught us bayonet fighting. That was something I enjoyed. All that aggression I'd been venting on the streets of Canberra was now allowed, even encouraged, to come to the fore. Singleton has a bayonet-assault course and the officer in charge told us he wanted controlled aggression all the way through, and he wanted to hear you. So as soon as he said 'Go!', everyone started screaming and hollering at the top of their lungs. At the beginning of the course was a big bear-pit filled with freezing-cold water. You had to run up, going '*Aaaaahhh!*' all the way, and jump in and swim through, with all your webbing on, while trying to keep your rifle out of the water. It was so cold, all the air got sucked from your lungs, but you waded out of there, still screaming as you went. Suddenly, you were crawling under barbed wire, trying not to have your skin ripped off but still going 100 kilometres an hour. To top it off, people shot blanks over your head like it was a war zone.

Then you got into the pits, where you did the bayonet fighting, and you were still screaming, with adrenalin coursing through your veins. They had tyres with big shooting-range pictures of soldiers on them and as you raced up to them, you screeched '*F-u-u-u-ck!*' It was absolutely insane. One time I got so totally caught up in it and ran so hard at the tyre, my bayonet got stuck. I didn't know what to do next, so I just kept booting the picture of the soldier in the head. I remember my corporal watching me, shaking his head and saying, 'Fucking hell, de Gelder, you're a maniac!'

We also learnt how to properly shoot rifles, light machine-guns, rocket launchers and how to employ claymores – the anti-personnel mines that can explode on command or by trip-wire. We also learnt how to fire a M79 grenade-launcher, the old single-shot shoulder-fired weapon they used in the Vietnam War. These days it's been replaced by the M203, or as we Aussies call it the GLA – Grenade Launcher Attachment – which is designed to attach to the underside of a rifle. Like any boy I'd always been fascinated by weapons, and this felt, much like those strippers, like another young male fantasy.

I'd begun enjoying myself. I'd found a bit of a niche, I got to do lots of PT, there was plenty of free food and I was hanging out with my new mates. There'd always been nothing better than spending time with my friends, and in the army it was just the same. I still kept in touch with my old friends but formed strong bonds with the guys I was training with; there were people from every background imaginable and from all over Australia. That was awesome. You were mixing with those you might never have expected to meet in your ordinary life and it felt like a whole new world was opening up. I also enjoyed learning new skills and pushing myself ever harder. Even the discipline wasn't as much of an irritant. I think I just changed over time, and it gradually became part of everyday life.

We trained hard, worked hard and were ridden like a Christmas favourite most of the time, so weekends off you'd spend around the base, trying to make yourself feel human again. You'd go to the supermarket to buy baby wipes so you could clean yourself up when you were out bush, or buy rations for the next trip out field, and just have some normal food – which you'd actually be able to eat slowly. Much as I enjoyed being with my new mates, I also liked my own company, and would often head off to watch a movie by myself or walk around Singleton seeing the sights. But you'd inevitably end the evenings in a pub, and sometimes in a fight or two.

We had a sergeant in our platoon, an old-school soldier, who'd served in some really shit war zones in his time, like Bosnia and Somalia. He'd line us up on the parade ground on a Friday arvo and say, 'Okay, men, you've had a good week, now I want you to go out tonight and get pissed and fuck fat chicks. If anyone comes up and tries to have a go at you, I don't want you to get into any fights. But if they start them, I want you to beat the shit out of them.' The corporals would be standing behind him, just shaking their heads in despair. But he never seemed to notice. His first question on a Monday morning would be, 'So, who fucked some fat chicks?' There were always a few big grins and paws in the air.

At the end of IET they organised our postings. We were given a list and told to write down which battalion we wanted. Then the officer in charge said, 'Hands up anyone who'd jump out of a plane.' I put my hand up immediately. So, without any more discussion, I was posted straight to 3 RAR (Parachute), a rapid deployment light-infantry unit that makes up a major slice of Australia's Ready Deployment Force and who've seen active service everywhere – Japan, Korea, in the old Malaya, Vietnam, East Timor, the Solomon Islands, Afghanistan, Iraq . . . the lot. I was to be based at Holsworthy Barracks in southwest Sydney, and was going to become a paratrooper.

The battalion 3 RAR is well known the world over for its courage under fire. Formed in 1948, it came to international attention during the Korean War in the 1950s. 3 RAR was the first Australian Army unit in action in Korea and, with other United Nations troops, had advanced as far as the Kapyong Valley on a key route south of the capital Seoul when the Chinese launched a major offensive. Despite being heavily outnumbered and battered by wave after wave of sustained attacks, 3 RAR held its position, wearing out and dispiriting the enemy, and was still on the front line when the fighting ended. For that the soldiers were awarded the US Presidential Citation. Their original barracks in South Australia and their current one in Holsworthy have been called the Kapyong Lines ever since. While I'd been training in Singleton I'd seen some of the 3 RAR paratroopers in their maroon berets, the symbolic headgear for paratroopers the world over. I'd felt awe and admiration. When I arrived at the Kapyong Lines and finally received my beret, I felt ten foot tall and bulletproof.

Yet in some ways becoming a paratrooper was a baptism of fire. Up until that point the only older people around were senior to you and in charge of your training. All of a sudden you were with a lot of people older than you who weren't particularly interested in your wellbeing. Many were keen to remind the new ones, and particularly the new young ones, of their position on the lowest rung. Some would even pick on them, but happily it didn't happen much to me as I was a bit older than most of the new boys. I was grateful. Even the nickname they gave me – 'Dutchie', in recognition of my de Gelder heritage – wasn't so bad. I guess it's natural to feel a bit nervous when you go into a new environment, but you hold your head high, push your shoulders back and hope for the best. What's going to happen usually does, no matter what you do.

At Holsworthy one of the first things the new guys have to do is what's called a 'shat special'. We had a boozer at the back of the barracks, a pub run by soldiers for soldiers. There an old military policeman's helmet was filled up with two shots of everything behind the bar and topped up with Guinness. As a newcomer you have to stand on the table and skol the whole thing while everyone sings the battalion song. You're not allowed to stop. Then you've got to carry the helmet around the whole night and everyone you walk past has to pour beer into it to keep it topped up.

The night I did it I don't remember a single thing. But everyone else did. Apparently, every time I walked up the two stairs to get into the bar, I didn't noticed the glass doors were closed, so I'd walk straight into the glass, bounce off, fall down the steps, then climb up them again, walk into the glass, bounce off, fall down . . . and on and on it went. But, comparatively speaking, I didn't come off too badly. After all, I'd had a lot of practice with stupid behaviour.

At other times, when the older soldiers wanted someone to drink with at the pub and their mates were away, they'd just go to the room of a new guy – easily identifiable by the traditional slouch hat, or 'crap hat', a newbie wore – kick in the door and order him to the pub. He might protest and say he didn't want to drink, but they'd insist, referring to his hat and saying, 'Let's go, lid. You're fucking coming to the pub!'

Drinking is a big part of army life; it's almost endorsed by the forces. They believe it builds bonds and strengthens mateship. That was fine by me. Clearly, I'd enjoyed a drink since my teens, and in the army the booze was good and cheap. But that kind of drinking culture does have a darker side. There are some people who end up alcoholics and the Australian Defence Force has a thing called 'the Tank' where they send these people. We had a civvy come to talk to my platoon one day about excessive drinking. She said that any more than four drinks in a row was considered binge drinking. We all looked at each other and laughed; four wasn't even a good warm-up. But while we'd still go out drinking most nights, I gradually learned control and moderation. The physical demands of army life taught you best. If you drank yourself silly, you just couldn't perform the next day. Always enjoying competition, I was getting used to the feeling of being one of the best at everything.

When it came to daily work, it was training for what the battalion was all about. In theory the special forces go in and find out where the enemy and all their gear are, and then we're flown in, thrown out of a plane 20, 30 or 40 kilometres away, before walking to the airfield, killing the enemy, and finally taking control of the airfield so our planes can land and bring in other troops. Easy!

Our first course was at the army's Parachute Training School at the Fleet Air Arm's base *HMAS Albatross*, near Nowra, two hours south of Sydney. There we had to do a fitness test, with chin-ups, a run, push-ups and sit-ups, before starting the three-week session. There were three phases to it: aircraft drills, where we learned what to do inside the plane before we jumped out; flight drills, where we learned how to fall; and landings, where we learned how not to die when you hit the ground, otherwise known as 'spearing in' or 'crumping'.

No one did particularly well at the flight part initially, because we had to practise in a harness with straps, or risers, which dangled down from the roof and went between your legs. The straps were old, made out of slippery nylon, and they crushed your balls as you just hung there in agony. Some blokes have been known to actually pass out from the combination of pain and residual alcohol from the night before. Then, finally, when it was time, you had to pull your whole body weight up one riser and hold yourself at 90 degrees – you shook with the effort – and then release and throw the risers away, falling about two feet with the straps jamming up between your legs. It really wasn't much fun.

The kind of jumping we did is called 'static line jumping'; it's designed for jumps from low heights, at something like 1000 feet, where you can actually see the bark on the trees. The aim is to get you from the plane to the ground as fast as possible without dying or getting shot, and it's more a matter of falling in an upright

TOP : Playing happy families, 1991: left to right, my youngest brother Sean, Dad, me, Jacqui, Mum and Travis

BOTTOM : Taking time out with my favourite hobby: skateboarding. Here posing for a photo with icy poles and my mates Tim (left) and Ben (middle).

TOP : The wild boys in Canberra, 1997: Me on the right, with my mates Snowy and Lez, having a drink and a few smokes

RIGHT : Starting out on a whole new path in 2000. The Australian Army's newest recruit.

TOP : Bayonet training at Singleton, 2001. My corporal told me I was a maniac.

BOTTOM : On bush patrol in East Timor, taking a quick meal break, mid-2002

TOP : CDAT – the hardest audition of my life. Here, we had to perform endless push-ups on the sand before yet another 4km swim. I'm closest to the camera, February 2005
BOTTOM : Taking time out for a beer after a day of mine-clearing off the coast of Tioman Island, Malaysia, 2008

OPPOSITE TOP : Exhibit number one – going through the paces in a clearance-diver display in Canberra, 2008
[INSET] One of the great love affairs of my life – my Aprilia RSVR 1000, my big V twin Italian sports bike. Later, it broke my heart to sell it.

CLEARANCE DIVING BRANCH

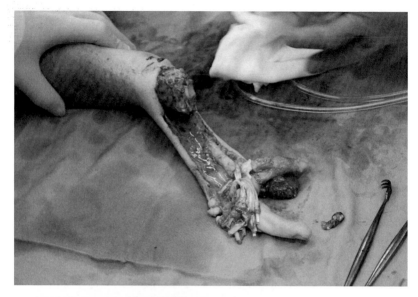

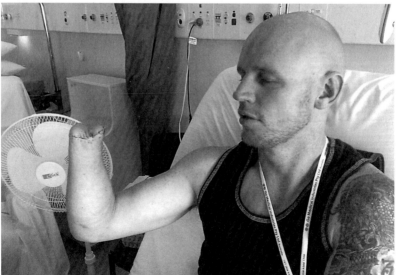

TOP : February 2009: What was left of my right hand after the shark attack. You can see just the thumb and one finger and some empty skin. There was nothing the doctors could do. Gruesome photos courtesy of my great doc – thanks mate! – Dr Kevin Ho.

BOTTOM : I came to terms very quickly with losing my hand. From the moment I realised the shark had taken it, I accepted the fact and concentrated on saving my leg.

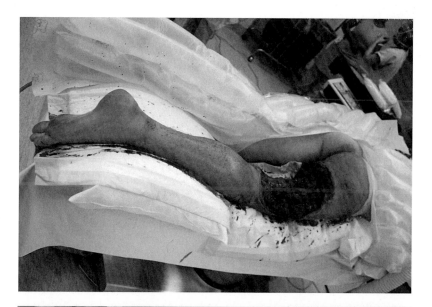

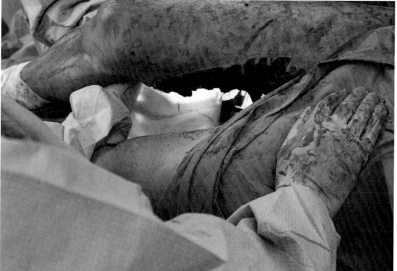

TOP : While it took a huge chomp out of the back of my leg, luckily, it missed a major blood vessel by just a couple of millimetres. Had it got that, I would have bled to death there and then in the water.

BOTTOM : The shark's teethmarks are plainly visible on what was left of the back of my right leg. It tore out most of my sciatic nerve, the biggest peripheral nerve in the body.

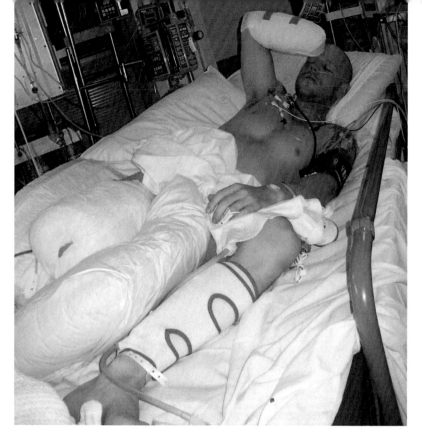

TOP : I made the decision to have my leg amputated very quickly, as soon as I was told I could be up and running on a prosthetic within the year. But I had a terrible reaction to the drugs straight after the operation. That was probably my darkest moment.
BOTTOM : After the amputation of my leg, the top of it swelled up like a balloon. I was meant to wait until the swelling had completely gone down before I was allowed to have a prosthetic fitted but I was so impatient, I persuaded them it didn't hurt at all. I lied.

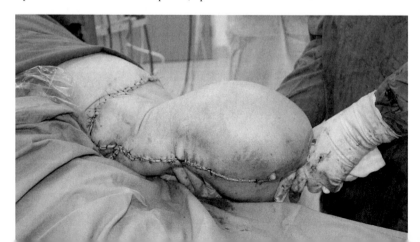

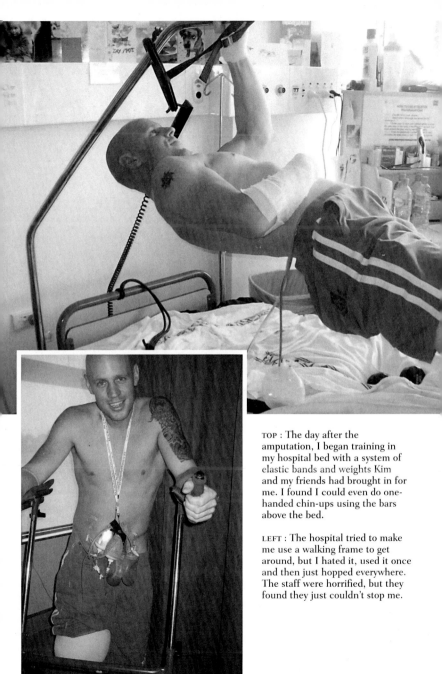

TOP : The day after the amputation, I began training in my hospital bed with a system of elastic bands and weights Kim and my friends had brought in for me. I found I could even do one-handed chin-ups using the bars above the bed.

LEFT : The hospital tried to make me use a walking frame to get around, but I hated it, used it once and then just hopped everywhere. The staff were horrified, but they found they just couldn't stop me.

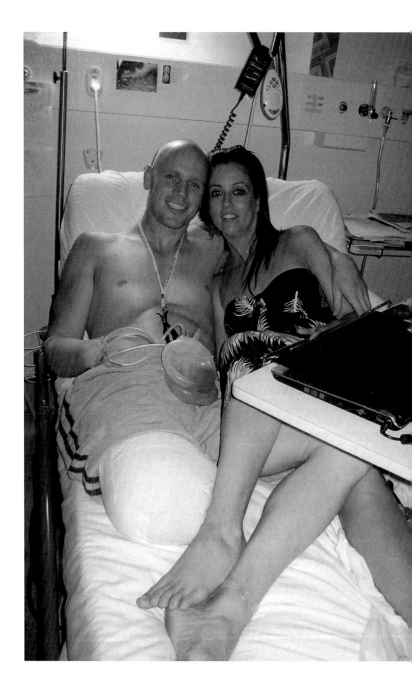

PAGE OPPOSITE : My girlfriend Kim stayed by my side the whole time I was in hospital. Some of the nurses didn't approve!

TOP : As soon as I was allowed to leave hospital on April 15 2009, my friends threw me a 'I'm Still Alive!' party at Bronte Beach. The beer tasted twice as good as I'd ever remembered BOTTOM : I went along to a hydrotherapy pool with a physio to see how I'd cope. After that, I just went to the beach and swam in the sea by myself or with my mates. I thought that'd be much better for me.

TOP : I resumed training in earnest, toughening up the stump on my arm to bear my weight and working with my prosthetic leg to work out how best to do push-ups. June 2009.
BOTTOM : February 2010 – one year on from the shark attack. It was an anniversary worth drinking to with my mates at a friend's wedding. Left to right, Morgan, Dalla, Brock, me and Lez.

TOP : Back in the deep end. *60 Minutes'* Peter Overton took me swimming with sharks at Oceanworld, Manly. The first time a 3-metre shark swam over me, I felt a shiver. April 2010. Photo courtesy Stephen Taylor, *60 Minutes*

BOTTOM : We've since become good friends. He's an enormously likeable bloke — even while trying to feed me to sharks . . . again. Photo courtesy Stephen Taylor

TOP : Made it! I finished the annual charity fundraiser, the Sydney Tower Run-Up, in a very respectable 18 minutes and 55 seconds. Not bad for 1504 steps. July 2010. Photo courtesy Leading Seaman Jules Amos

OPPOSITE TOP : Getting back on a surf board felt so good. It was tricky standing up at first on a leg you can't feel, but it didn't take too long to get to grips with it. June 2010. Photo courtesy the TV show *Manly Surf*, 5 Oceans Media

OPPOSITE BOTTOM : On a break in Queensland I tried skydiving – and loved that too. I'm never happier than when facing new challenges, and never more frustrated than when others try to stop me. September 2010.

These days I look forward to whatever the future may bring with confidence and excitement. Life's good. At the park near my home on Sydney's northern beaches with my dogs, ridgeback-cross-mastiff Chip and mastiff-cross-boxer Bonnie. February 2011. Photo courtesy Jimmy Thomson position than the graceful float down of actual parachuting. Your parachute's hooked onto a yellow cord that runs over your shoulder to a steel cable that sits along the length of the plane. So when you jump, the cord feeds out in zigzags all the way across your backpack and when it gets to the end, the parachute instantly comes out. It means the parachute is deployed immediately after you've jumped from the plane, regardless of your own actions.

I was so excited when it came time for my first jump. I'd never done anything like it before. When it finally happened, it was so exhilarating and a huge rush. You come in fast, falling at a rate of 4.6–6.4 metres per second, but you only tend to hurt yourself if you don't do the correct drills. Luckily, I was never injured. Plenty were. Later, when we did exercises in Queensland, around 35 people fractured their shins, or broke their knees, ankles, even their backs. Another time one of my mates experienced what's called a 'Roman candle', when the lines all get tangled up so that the parachute doesn't fill out properly, and he ended up with a compressed bunch of vertebrae. On another exercise one friend was left hanging upside down, stuck in a tree, and another crash-landed on his own pack.

I had a lot of mates who absolutely hated the jumps, and a lot of people got sick on the planes beforehand as well. We did another trip up to Townsville in a C130 Hercules, which are notorious for being incredibly slow, and it took hours and hours. It was claustro-phobic, hot, we were cramped up in the tiny spaces on benches, our packs in front of us and our helmets in our laps while all the way up the pilots were practising tactical flying, so they were going up and down constantly. Many of the guys were throwing up into their helmets, then looking alarmed as they realised they'd soon have to put them back on their heads for their jumps.

By the time those jumps came round everyone was totally over it. But we were suddenly standing up, hooking on with the parachutes on our backs, the reserve chutes on our fronts and 40–50-kilogram packs attached to our legs. It was the middle of the night and no one really wanted to jump – doing night jumps is like stepping through a black door into nowhere, you can't see anything. But we'd all been in that plane so long, it was stifling and stank of spew, and we all wanted to get out into the fresh air whatever way we could.

As soon as you've jumped at night, you're too busy going through your drills to think about anything else – making sure you've got no tangles, looking out for anyone underneath you and searching for silhouettes in the darkness. The only way you can tell where the ground is, is to pull a cord that drops your pack down on a six-foot rope and listen out for the thud when it hits the ground. That's when you know you're nearly there. When you see the ground, you want to reach for it, which is the worst possible thing you can do. It means you instinctively straighten your knees and point your toes, then when you hit the ground, your knees go out backwards or sideways. So you just wait, see the ground, assume the correct position with legs slightly bent at the knee, chin tucked in and hands pulling down on the risers in front of your face to protect your head and then close your eyes. As soon as you hit the ground, you lie there, wriggle your toes and fingers and think, *Thank God! They still work!*

Then you stand up, pack up your parachute and get on with it.

# 11

## BLACK HAWK UP

It was one of the biggest military exercises ever to take place on Australian soil. In May 2001 Tandem Thrust was launched, a biannual bilateral training operation for Australian and US forces; this was a rehearsal of how we'd repel any invasion of Australia by a hostile foreign power. Set in the Shoalhaven area of NSW and around the Great Barrier Reef Marine Park in Queensland, it involved around 28 000 troops, 130 ships, 130 aircraft and count-less hundreds of military vehicles. The aim was for both teams to practise working together in conventional military operations, peacekeeping and disaster relief – on a massive scale.

I'd been in 3 RAR's Charlie Company for only a few months before I took part in Tandem Thrust. Our mission involved flying in, jumping out of a plane, then walking and walking and walking for days. Finally, we reached our destination, where we dug some pits along the side of a hill, and then walked and walked some more. But just as I was heartily ruing the whole thing, we were given the good news: we had to get into a series of Black Hawks to be taken somewhere else.

I'd never been in a helicopter before, let alone a Black Hawk, and I was very excited. The four-bladed twin-engine Black Hawk is incredibly powerful – capable of carrying 11 soldiers with equipment, lifting 1170 kilograms of cargo internally or 4050 kilograms externally with a sling – and it's used for all sorts of front-line missions. Just standing on the landing zone, watching the Black Hawk swoop in and hearing the roar of its engines gave me a thrill. I was in absolute awe of its power and grace.

Climbing in, I felt my heart really start to race. I harnessed myself into the seat and then felt her lift off, as light as a bird. You could feel the tremendous power throbbing and vibrating all the way through your body; it was an amazing feeling. Looking down, I could see the green of the mountain ranges in the bush outside Townsville roll out before me and on the other side, the golden beaches of the coast wind past. I looked at my mates and they were all looking at me.

'What's the matter?' I asked them. They laughed.

'It's you,' one of them replied. 'You've got such a big stupid grin plastered all over your face.' I couldn't help it. This was what I'd hoped the army would be all about.

Finally, the ride was over. We landed in a plume of dust and grit and went back to walking. But it didn't seem so bad now. Even though we walked for a further two days and two nights straight, across really rough terrain, carrying 30-kilogram packs on our backs, holding machine-guns and navigating through the darkness using night-vision goggles, I still felt light on my feet from that chopper ride.

At one point we got a report that an enemy Leopard tank had been sighted in the area so we holed up in a dry river bed until the platoon sergeant shouted at us to start digging in. We'd been working hard for about an hour when we started to hear a slow rumble. Everyone stopped digging and listened intently. We were all trying to work out where it was coming from, while at the same time grabbing our weapons and taking fighting positions. As the noise grew louder we could do nothing but wait, expecting at any moment to see a huge tank come over the rise. The ground started to shake and all of a sudden a huge herd of brumbies came stampeding into the river 10 metres from our position. There were so many of them that if they'd landed in the river bed on top of us, there wouldn't have been much of us left. But it was a beautiful sight.

After that exercise was over we went back to Holsworthy and continued all our training. Some of it was fun; some of it not so much. The basic and specialist communications were all right, but I preferred things like the close-quarters fighting course, where you learned about fighting other people to take their weapons off them. It's a bit like martial arts, where you're using people's weight against them, putting them in wrist locks and joint locks to disarm them, and throwing them. It used a number of the moves I'd picked up as a teenager from Muay Thai and I loved getting back to that physicality, although this time with a lot more discipline. I learned how controlling your moves and your aggression

enabled you to be a much more effective fighter than I'd been
on the streets of Canberra, and how not to get hurt when others
attacked you. There was so much there I wished I'd known as
a kid. During that course I found myself working from 7 a.m.
to 7 p.m. and spending most of my day getting thrown on my
head and back. The next morning when I'd wake up, everything
hurt – just like in the old days. But the difference was that this
time it all felt worth it.

I was enjoying everything so much more than at Kapooka and
Singo. Now we were really learning about life on the front line;
we were being paid a lot more and we weren't getting yelled at
as much. Of course, everything was harder and took longer but
usually you'd knock off at 4 p.m. and then your life was your own.
Not all of my mates who came through agreed. By the third year,
three of the other five guys from my intake had done runners,
one of them with a girl I'd been seeing! I guess it just wasn't for
them. But I'd realised there was a lot more to life than what I'd
known before: I was being exposed to a huge variety of people
and stories and knowledge. I felt I was really growing up.

After a year and a half at Holsworthy I was deployed on my first
overseas operation – to East Timor, the troubled nation to our north.
In the 25 years since its 1975 occupation by Indonesia, around
18 600 of its people had been killed and a further 84 200 had died
from starvation or illness. Three years after the international peacekeeping force went in and the UN took over the country, our role
now was to protect the East Timorese. My posting started in April
2002, just a month before independence was finally formalised,
and Xanana Gusmao was sworn in as the country's first president.

Before we left for the six-month posting, I put my hand up to do a two-week course in the Timorese language, Tetum, and when we arrived, I turned out to be the only one who could speak it. I was appointed the platoon translator, which was very cool, and whenever the boss went to speak to a village chief, I went along and had a chat. One time we were at a village where the locals hadn't seen white people for ages. We bought a chicken from them and they invited us back for dinner in the chief's hut. During the evening they told me that the chicken's head was a delicacy. When it was offered to me, I reluctantly went to take a bite – until I noticed the whole village standing outside, looking through a hole in the thatching, laughing their arses off. They'd decided it'd be funny to mess with us. Next, they gave me what they called a 'sun ball'. It looked innocuous enough, just like a mini lime. It was only when I popped it into my mouth and started crying, coughing and blubbering that I realised it was filled with chillies. I think I provided them enough entertainment to last the month.

My time there, spent constantly on the move from place to place, going on patrols by foot or in armoured personnel carriers, sleeping out, and with only my own clothes, weapons and equipment, was a whole new education for me about life beyond Australia. East Timor is one of the poorest countries in the world but I was so surprised by its people. They had nothing, yet they always seemed so happy. I'd see the women sweeping the leaves out of their dirt-floor huts and they always stopped to smile and say hello. It was humbling.

But the poverty could also be heartbreaking. Sometimes we'd

give the kids water and lollies, or pay them to fetch us coconuts. Then we'd buy little rugs and trinkets from their parents to help them out. Some begged for the chance to go through our rubbish, but we were under strict orders to burn it. As soon as you drove away you could see people coming out from the jungle dressed in rags and trying to put out the flames and then, with socks on their hands to protect them, raking through what was left to see what could be salvaged.

One of our main tasks was protecting the East Timorese from armed units of the Indonesian military, the TNI, who might cross the border from West Timor and just go on the rampage, killing and looting. It felt good to be finally putting our skills and every-thing we'd learned to a good cause. It was the first time I really felt like a representative of Australia and of the army, and I took great pride in that. I stood tall.

At one place where we were patrolling the border there were reports of TNI soldiers coming in and taxing the locals at the markets. One of our tasks was to hide out in dense jungle and watch the markets just 200 metres away. It was surprisingly hard work lying in the thick undergrowth, day after day, watching and waiting, barely able to move in case you were spotted. Eventually, we saw one guy in TNI trousers snatching money from a woman and yelling at her, so we radioed in and were told to take him. We jumped out of that jungle, camouflage paint on, filthy, dirty and angry, brandishing our guns and shouting. The woman looked at us and looked at him, and a big smile spread over her face. He was terrified and dropped to his knees with his hands in the air.

The TNI had spread rumours that Australian soldiers ate

babies and this guy was rigid with fear at what we might do to him. But we just took him back to our platoon in the hills, where he knelt down and bawled his eyes out and prayed. Our commanding officer later handed him back to the TNI commanding officer, who slapped him and threw him to the ground. I think it was punishment less for taxing the locals than for being caught doing it.

We'd also sometimes watch the TNI at night on the other side of the river border with our thermal-imaging goggles. We'd see the hookers come down to the water's edge and the soldiers having a bit of fun with them before going back to work. They weren't the most disciplined of fighting forces.

At Maliana, 150 kilometres southwest of the capital, Dili, I did a couple more courses. One was a communications course, and the other was the preselection for a sniper course we could take back at Holsworthy. The first test for that was in camouflage and concealment, where you had to hide using foreground cover, rear-ground cover, middle cover, divots in the ground, whatever you could, like a grown-ups' game of hide-and-seek. I found a great spot on the ground where I could see my seeker but was completely hidden from view. All of a sudden I felt a little tickle on my stomach, but of course I couldn't move. Then I felt another and another and they were actually beginning to hurt. Gradually, the pain spread from my stomach to my chest to my neck. I lay there in agony, but I so wanted to get on to that snipers' course, I didn't dare even twitch. Finally, the seeker called to me to show myself and I leapt to my feet, only to discover I'd been lying on an ants' nest. They'd swarmed to attack me and I was bitten everywhere; even my belly button was so swollen it had closed. Everyone else had a good laugh about it.

Another of the exercises was navigation in the bush. I paired up with a mate and carried the radio. Geographically, East Timor is full of rugged mountain ranges, interspersed with high plateaus, areas of rainforest, eucalyptus thickets, and roads and paths often destroyed by the retreating TNI. So it's not the easiest of places to find your way around. But we set out with our maps to navigate past all the right checkpoints along the way. The problem was the maps weren't fantastically accurate and following the straight track of the compass was hard because there were so many gullies and creeks, so we decided to cut around them and come up the other side. Bright idea. Before long, we'd got completely lost.

About three hours later base came over on the radio to ask us our location.

'I have no idea,' I answered.

'What the fuck do you mean, you have no idea?' came the voice back.

'I really don't know where we are,' I said. I was mortified. 'We've been walking for a while now . . .'

The response was unsympathetic.

'Well, you bloody well work it out and radio back to me straightaway!'

After a few minutes, we spotted a big concrete slab on the ground.

'I've seen that before!' I said to the guy with me. 'I'm sure of it.' We walked up to the slab, looked out over the nearest hill and the base was right in front of us. We'd actually walked in a huge circle. But we didn't tell anyone. We both wanted to pass that selection course too much.

Part of our work while in East Timor was forming the security detachment for one of the intelligence platoons high up on a mountain. We were always having to shake scorpions off our packs and one of my mates, on a trip to relieve himself in the middle of the night, was bitten by a snake. We applied a pressure immobilisation bandage, marked the time and position of the bite on it and then, as I was on communications, I got on the radio and called in a medivac for him. The trouble was, I was standing too close to the landing zone we'd marked out for the chopper in infra-red Cyalume glow sticks and when it arrived, the power of its downthrust blew me off my feet and sent me rolling backwards all the way down the hill. In addition, it turned out to have been a bite from a bamboo viper, so we shouldn't have bandaged it tightly, either. As soon as the medics took the bandage off, the venom went straight into my mate's muscles. I think it was painful at the time, but he was fine in the end, happily.

The remoteness of the area and the ruggedness of the terrain made it difficult to do everything right much of the time. Patrolling the West Timorese border one day, we got a little bit what we call 'geographically embarrassed' about where the boundary was – it's a river but it drains away to nothing in some places – so we accidentally invaded Indonesia. That, had anyone found out about it, could well have become a serious international incident. Luckily, it's still a tightly kept secret.

# 12

## IMPROVISE, ADAPT AND OVERCOME

By now I'd started to understand the true meaning and value of the mantra used by both the Australian Army and the US Marine Corps: improvise, adapt and overcome. They intended it to apply to any job at hand: think creatively, and be flexible and determined to get it done, whatever the odds. But gradually, I'd begun to use the motto for my own life too.

If you found yourself stuck in some God-awful circumstance or other, then it would be up to you to improvise to make the best of the situation. If that wasn't an option, then you'd have to adapt. And if those kinds of compromises were impossible, then the onus was on you to overcome – by either changing the situation to suit yourself, or getting the hell out and building a better life for yourself elsewhere.

At last I was beginning to understand that it was up to me to determine how my life turned out. If I'd carried on drifting as I did in my early years, I could so easily have ended up in prison or dead. Now that I'd at last found something of value I enjoyed doing, I could see I'd wasted all the years that had gone before, and started to regret it. Time is precious, gone in a flash, and far too valuable to fritter away getting pissed and stoned. Perhaps I could have achieved so much more if I'd applied myself earlier instead of fucking around for so long. It had taken me a long time to learn how to start really living, instead of just biding my time.

Growing up can be like walking through a maze filled with booby traps, with dead ends, wrong turns and false leads. More often than not, you'll make a bad decision, hit a trip-wire and what feels like the weight of the world will come tumbling down on top of you. Ultimately, everyone makes their own decisions and has to live with the repercussions, but then again, if you never made mistakes, then you'd never really learn how to live. It was just a shame I spent so much time making mistakes, and so little time learning from them.

You might not be good at school, you might not be good at the first few jobs you try, but I'd learned that in the end there was always something else you could do, always something else you could try until you found something you loved. You just had to find what you were passionate about, and then really run with it.

Changing the course of your life can certainly be tough at times. A lot of the things I was doing in the military, like shooting rockets, grenade-launchers and machine-guns, weren't a natural progression for someone who'd been working behind a bar. But hell, it's important to put yourself outside your comfort zone from time to time – how else are you ever going to discover what you can do when you're up against it? The next step is to learn to enjoy the challenge, the adrenalin, the excitement, the thrill. If you're scared of something, that's not a reason *not* to do it; it's all the more reason to do it. Some people might notice their weaknesses and shy away from doing something they're not good at. But if you're afraid of something, what you should be doing is bringing it closer to you. Knowledge dispels fear.

The army taught me that I shouldn't be scared of failure. Failure can be good; it's how you learn. After a while, I came to much prefer doing something myself, failing at it, learning from my mistakes, and trying again. I felt it was better to make mistakes at the start, so you didn't make them later when it was more important. I certainly behaved badly when I was younger, but hopefully I'd learned something from it, at least, and somehow become a better person.

### Matt

I encouraged Paul to join the defence forces as I thought the structure would be good for him but, to be honest, I never thought he'd last long. I also worried a bit: he was one of the clumsiest people I've known in my whole life. When we were kids, my mum would always give him a plastic cup to drink out of rather than a glass. When we lived together, I had a set of 12 wine glasses. Within six months, Paul had broken 11 of them. We were talking about the army and I thought, *Holy crap! He'll be holding a gun!*

But when he joined, it was as if he had a purpose for the

first time. It gave him the direction his life had been lacking up to that point. He really thrived, and loved it. Before, he'd always been skinny, but in the army he started putting on a bit of weight and getting a lot more self-confident. I think the blokey environment was good for him too. He became much more outgoing.

He started striving to achieve things. Since he'd always been competitive, he loved trying to outdo the other guys. He began to want to be the best he possibly could be at everything he did, and he gave it 100 per cent.

Back home in Australia, after the stint in East Timor, I was trying to put into practice everything I felt I'd now learned. I'd moved out of barracks as the accommodation there was being refurbished and we were offered rental assistance to live outside, so I rented an apartment in Sydney's south. I wasn't terribly successful with women at that stage since I was still so skinny and weedy but I was in a relationship then and I later moved out to live with the girl. It proved a disaster. Suddenly, I was being asked to account for where I was and what I was doing 24 hours a day – it was like being back with my parents. We broke up and got back together a total of three times before I finally moved back in with mates.

I tried to come to terms with my past a bit more too. My sister, Jacqui, had her 18th birthday party back in Canberra so I went home with a couple of the guys from the army base to help her celebrate. It was the first time I'd seen my dad since I left home. We said hello, then he went out and returned with an esky full of beer. We had a couple of drinks together and talked, and I think that's the first time we'd done so, man to man. We didn't actually say much though. Dad has spent his whole career trying to be unassuming and in the background, and I'd never been a great conversationalist. But we felt comfortable together.

After a few weeks working back at Holsworthy, I was sent on a three-week trip to a training centre in Canungra, about an hour inland from the Gold Coast, which had originally been built to train Vietnam-bound soldiers in jungle-fighting techniques. After learning how to patrol and fight in jungle conditions, we had to do an obstacle course there. It was so hardcore, one year a football team point-blank refused to even have a go. The first time I saw it I instantly felt nervous. But by telling myself what a great challenge it would be, I made myself get excited at the prospect of trying it out.

I'd been pretty good at the obstacle course at Singleton, often going last and helping the slow ones over the walls, but still always managing to catch up to finish first. This course looked a completely different prospect, however. At the start was an eight-foot rope to climb up, with another stretching over water. On the other side you had to climb back down, then crawl through a 15-foot corrugated-iron tunnel half submerged in water so freezing cold, you were hyperventilating before you'd even entered it. Because you were dressed in full camouflage gear, and laden with webbing, ammunition, rifles and machine-guns, you had to lie down on your back in the water and squeeze yourself head first and upside down into the tunnel, pulling your way through. Halfway through, the little air pocket you started with disappeared, until you had no air left to breathe. Some guys were panicking as they went through and dropped their rifles. They then had to go through a second time to retrieve them – or beg someone else to do it for them.

At the other end there were big tyre chicanes you had to race through, barbed wire and walls to jump over, a 15-foot wall with a rope on one side to help you climb up, and another one equally high with no rope that you'd have to form a human pyramid to get over, with the guy at the top reaching down and pulling the next guy up. Then at the end there was a tower from which you jumped into the river. By the end of it all, you were absolutely busted. But it was awesome!

### Sean de Gelder

I didn't think Paul would last in the army, especially since he'd never really been a sporty person – apart from the kickboxing. But everyone I spoke to who knew him there said how good and how fit he was. That was a bit of a shock.

He was always someone who wanted to do his own thing. So when he got to do it, he was determined to do it really well.

Now in Alpha Company – just the first of the alphabet: Alpha, Bravo, Charlie, Delta, etc – we flew out to Noumea on an exercise where we had to board a French patrol boat, evacuate an island of supposedly foreign nationals, and secure the area. On our way there the seas were huge, with massive waves, and the bow of the ship kept plunging straight down under the water and then rearing back up. While nearly everyone else immediately started throwing up, I discovered it didn't affect me. Even better, it meant a big feed – of mine and everyone else's lunch serves. Then, with a couple of other guys, I went out on the bridge of the boat, waited for the rush of water, and slid straight down the wings. After each ride, I'd climb back up for another go. Eventually, we were spotted by some officers, who were horrified at what we were doing. They yelled at us in French and we were confined inside.

It was a fun exercise – although we did get into a bit of a scuffle with the French soldiers who were playing the enemy and wouldn't do as they were told. But the most interesting thing about it for me was my first experience with navy clearance divers. While we were still a way offshore they started bringing all their diving gear to the deck so they could swim out to check if there were any enemy soldiers on the beach. Later that day I saw them again, cruising around in their shorts with their guns, looking cool.

'Jeez!' I said to the next bloke, 'that looks like a nice job!' After those two overseas exercises, I was longing for a bit more adventure, something different from all the walking and digging and hunting for an invisible enemy. I thought I'd found it one day when, while practising fire and movement techniques in the Belanglo State Forest – famous for the site of the Ivan Milat backpacker murders – my sergeant handed me his mobile, saying there was a call for me from the platoon commander.

'Dutchie,' he said, 'I've got a question for you. Do you want to go to the desert?' I didn't hesitate.

'Fucking A, sir!' I replied. 'Of course I do.'

It turned out I was one of five guys selected to go over to Iraq on a security detachment, or sec det, to bolster the number of soldiers already there. I was thrilled. We did some pre-deployment training, got issued with all the gear and were given country and defence briefings, books about Iraq and CDs on Arabic so we could practise phrases. I got straight into it and started learning as much as I could. But four days before we were meant to go, we were suddenly told it was all off. Apparently, the chief of army didn't want to send anyone for less than three months, and we were scheduled to be there for just two and a half. We were all absolutely gutted, but the army's not the sort of environment where you can argue against decisions like that. You just have to do what you're told.

That was the start of me feeling a little bit disillusioned with army life. I'd been there for four years, trained as hard as I could, and done everything that was asked of me, but now I was being sent back to the tedium of Holsworthy. It felt like I was constantly training, training, training, yet never seeing any action. It had been the greatest adventure of my life and I knew I didn't want to leave the defence forces, but I did want something new. It felt like it was time for a change.

Change seemed to be happening all around me in any case. My mum called me one day to say she and Dad were separating after 32 years of marriage. She said they hadn't been happy together for a long time; they both wanted different things out of life. I was pleased for them both. Ever since I was a kid, I remembered them fighting. In retrospect I'd spent a whole lot of time in my childhood knowing my parents were staying together only for the sake of their four kids, and I don't think that's a healthy thing for a kid to know. When she broke the news, I think Mum was uncertain about what my reaction would be. It was simple. 'Thank God!' I said.

Now it felt like my turn to change. I talked to a few of my mates in the platoon. One of them confessed he was feeling over the army and that he was applying to join the clearance divers. I was intrigued. He was really excited about it – and he was someone who never got excited about *anything*. I started wondering what life as a diver might be like.

As it turned out I didn't have to wait for long to find out. Soon after that I was sent on yet another training course. This time it was helicopter underwater-escape training – for anyone going to be on a helicopter that will fly over water. It starts with you, fully clothed, being locked into a mock helicopter that's submerged in water, turned upside down and with all the lights switched off – leaving you to get out in under a certain amount of time. Some people freaked out but I felt quite comfortable. I held my breath for 30 seconds, opened my eyes under the water to check everyone was out of my way, took off my belt and just climbed out of the window.

One of the safety supervisors there was a clearance diver and we started chatting about his job. The more he told me, the more it sounded like something I'd love to do. The Royal Australian Navy clearance divers are one of the defence forces' most specialised and highly regarded elite forces, sometimes dubbed the SAS of the underwater world. They can work at significant depths, sometimes in wild seas in the middle of nowhere in the pitch-black of night, and are expert in carrying out underwater battle-damage repairs on ships using hydraulic and explosive tools. They're also trained in combat, launching covert attacks behind enemy lines and taking part in secret counter-terrorism operations, sometimes employed in special-forces roles as part of the commando regiment's tactical assault group. In addition they find and dispose of bombs, and risk their lives to dismantle improvised explosive devices, similar to the action in the movie *The Hurt Locker*. The selection process is one of the most physically and mentally demanding of any defence force in the world.

I knew to stand even a chance I'd have to start training really hard. Only a handful of the hundreds of applicants every year from all over Australia get within a sniff of success. The trouble was, working as a paratrooper with the army, being sent on so many exercises, carrying heavy packs, sleeping rough and eating crap food with no time to train properly at the gym, I'd be pushing shit uphill. But then I came up with a plan: if I could get posted from Alpha Company to Delta Support Company, which ran the soldiers' store on base, I could pretty much run my own show – working there and training in my spare time specifically for the clearance divers' selection course. It seemed the perfect ruse.

But I hadn't taken into account my company commander, who kept refusing to let me go. Eventually, I discovered why – the swimming, cross-country and athletics carnivals were coming up and he knew I was one of the battalion's fastest swimmers and better athletes. I tried to think of a way around this, a way for us both to get what we wanted. A few days later I went to him with my proposal for a deal: if I helped them win, would he give me his blessing for a transfer?

The next week we won all three trophies and, suddenly, I was on my way.

# 13

## WHERE THE BLOODY HELL IS STARBOARD?

As soon as my partner staggered under my weight, I knew we had a problem. If I was going to have any chance of beating the other guys, I'd have to take drastic action. We were already ahead of the rest of the field of clearance diver applicants. I'd had my turn running along Sydney's Balmoral Beach, all 75 kilograms of me, with a fellow candidate, weighing in at 110 kilograms, over my shoulder in a fireman's carry. Now it was his turn to run with me. Since he'd started complaining of a sore back, things didn't look half as good.

'Stop right there!' I suddenly shouted to him as I slid back down off his shoulder. 'I want to win this thing.' I bent down in front of him. 'Now lean over me and I'll do the next leg.' I caught hold of him on my shoulder and did another lap of the beach, wading through knee-deep water to press home our advantage and finish first.

I was more determined than I'd ever been in my life before. And when you want something that much, it's amazing what strength and stamina you can summon. On the basis of my navy entrance-exam results and interview I'd been offered the chance to become an officer. But no thanks; what I wanted was the action of being a diver. The first step was to get through the three-week ships' divers course, and I was adamant that nothing and no one was going to slow me down – even the officer I'd been paired with, higher in rank than me, but nothing like as fit or fast.

Doing the course meant going back to getting yelled and screamed at all over again, but this time I took it in my stride. It helped that a lot of the sessions were fitness-oriented and we had to do hardcore PT every day, which I loved. While I'd never actually dived in my life before, that seemed to be coming naturally. I was comfortable in the water, and I had no worries with claustrophobia, being underwater or swimming at night. Even the long hours – from 7 a.m. to midnight or 2 a.m. many days – didn't particularly bother me. I saw all that as helping build up my endurance so I'd be ready for the selection tests to come.

By far the most difficult thing for me was taking in all the new knowledge. There was a lot of technical stuff to learn about diving, like the science behind it, the techniques, how to conduct mine-searches in deep water and how to check a ship's hull for mines and foreign objects, the health risks, the medical stuff like decompression illness, the regulations, the drills and all the signals you give to communicate with your colleagues both underwater and up on the surface.

While I'm quite a practical and logical-process kind of person,

I'm not great at academic learning, and I tend not to retain new facts easily. But the beauty is that I know my weaknesses, so I know I can combat them by studying hard, and doing things over and over again until I learn them. Others made it look easy, and I struggled, but then again I'm sure I made some of the physical stuff look like a breeze. It helped that on the course you were pushed with repeated questions. Even as you were swimming along, watching floats bob in the water and looking out for boat traffic to report, you were pumped for answers. There was no let-up on the intensity, and if you didn't get it right, you got push-up after push-up to do in groups of 50, or chin-ups, or those disappointed looks that somehow hurt even more. Finally, then, it would sink in.

I certainly didn't excel on the course. I just kept my head down, trying not to be noticed, and got through it. The whole navy stuff was new to me: working out what the bow was, what was aft, what a hawser was or an ebbing tide. It was a whole new language. Everyone else on the course, apart from one airforce guy, was from the navy – my mate who'd originally been considering the divers and suggested it to me had gone on to stay with the army and become a commando instead – so they were familiar with all the terms. They were standing there yelling out, 'Fenders outboard!' and 'Stand by lines starboard side two!' and I was thinking, *What's going on? What the fuck's a fender? Where the bloody hell is starboard?* They made allowances for me at first, but I knew I'd have to pick it up quickly, otherwise I'd soon be trying their patience.

Of course, the most effective way to learn is always by your mistakes, but that wasn't ideal here. At one point while I was treading water the dive supervisor told me to take a dive, so I immediately bent down from the hips, as I'd been taught, and went to use my body and my fins to propel myself downwards. It would have worked fine – except that I'd forgotten to dump the remaining air from my buoyancy compensator and no matter how hard I pulled with my hands or kicked with my legs, the lower half of my body just flapped around above the water like an epileptic seal. I kept it up for a little while, knowing what would be waiting for me on the surface. Eventually, I had to give up and, as my head popped out of the water, all I could hear was the supervisor yelling at me and everyone else pissing themselves with laughter.

At the end I was just incredibly relieved to have got through and I started immediately training even harder for the next stage, the ten-day Clearance Diving Acceptance Test (CDAT). Among the defence forces of the world, it's renowned for being one of the toughest and most gruelling physical, psychological and emotional ordeals anyone can put themselves through. I couldn't wait.

We started the first morning of the CDAT in February 2005 with 22 candidates, some of whom had been waiting years for the chance to try out. By that very same evening we were down to 18.

I wasn't surprised. Before I started I knew of the course's reputation. Already we'd run the 5-kilometre 'Gate to Gate', racing from the dive school at the bottom of the base up a steep incline to the front gate and then in a big loop around Sydney's North Shore. The run itself mightn't have been so bad but it was the Indian file, hill sprints, fireman's carries, push-ups, chin-ups, weights and a set of stairs that proved the real killers over the two and a half hour course. It didn't help either that we'd been pumped all along the route by dive-school staff intent on breaking us down physically and mentally. They told us we were useless, we didn't have a chance of succeeding and that we might as well give up now before the pain got any worse. At any moment we were free to get on the warm, comfortable minibus waiting to take us back to base. Why not get on now rather than later, when we'd be in too much pain to continue? In addition nobody was addressed by name; we were all simply referred to by a number, emblazoned on each of our yellow safety vests. You had to battle not to feel dehumanised and dispirited.

After we'd finished at nightfall, exhausted and sore, huffing and puffing with faces as red as beetroots and ready to do nothing more than drop on to our bunks and sleep like the dead, we were told to have a quick stretch because we were going to do it all again, starting immediately . . . Right there and then, two people handed in their vests and dropped out.

Yet every time someone relinquished their vest, I felt my resolve strengthen and I'd swear mine wouldn't be the next. We were constantly reminded of the toll the course took. The staff hung those vests where everyone could see them, like Indians collecting scalps. It scared some, and urged on others.

The next day the punishment was cranked up a notch. We spent six hours in the freezing water, swimming in a line across the harbour – and then were told to swim the 4 kilometres back again. We crawled into bed at 2 a.m., only to be woken four hours later and ordered out of bed and back into the harbour for our next exercise.

By then even more men had dropped out. It was the combination of physical exhaustion, the incredible psychological pressure and the confusion brought about by being barked at constantly and told to do complex tasks when you were too tired to concentrate on anything. All the while we were being watched by supervising officers writing notes about each one of us.

One day soon blurred into the next, in a feverish haze of runs – one 22 kilometres long – weights, push-ups and chin-ups, swimming, diving while holding your breath, tying knots, climbing up hillsides carrying sandbags that doubled as the bodies of wounded comrades, and lugging canoes 4 kilometres up rugged bush tracks to the top of mountains. You had constant kit musters, where you gathered all your gear, they called out the name of each item and you held it up and repeated the call and, if you did it too slowly, you were punished with push-ups. All through this you were still being expected to remain good humoured, valuing the team over yourself, neither too cocky nor too quiet and doing your very best to showcase your strength of character, while keeping a tight grasp of what remained of your sanity.

The exercises tested all our strengths and our weaknesses. Some people were good at running, but not at push-ups or heaves. Some could swim with fins on their feet like bloody dolphins, but struggled on the forced marches. All of us groaned at being woken at 2 a.m. to do a swim, then a forced march, with stairs and 80-kilogram stretcher-carries 10 kilometres uphill, and having to camp out. But whether it was a canoe paddle against the tide and wind for two hours, or a five-hour swim with fins from Mosman to Manly and back at 4 a.m., we did it together as a team. Our bond made us harder and stronger than we could ever be individually and, even though each day brought muscles close to the point of collapse, none of us wanted to let the staff win. These are the conditions that forge warriors and separate the inadequate from those you can trust with your life. Sleep deprivation mixed with the pressure of performing and constant mental and physical strain lets you see what a person is really capable of. Training combat-ready troops under such conditions is an essential element to building the finest and toughest. As the British wartime prime minister Winston Churchill once said, 'We sleep soundly in our beds because rough men stand ready in the night to visit violence on those who would do us harm.' I vowed to become one of those men.

That CDAT was the toughest thing I'd ever done. You were woken by all the lights going on and someone yelling at you. As soon as you were conscious, every muscle and bone and joint in your body would hurt, your nerves would jangle and your whole body would shake. But you'd drag your arse out of bed, hoping nothing was going to break, trying to draw strength from knowing that everyone else was suffering the same. The course was absolutely draining but you got no feedback at all, so you had no idea how you were doing until the last day. You were apprehensive, anxious and scared shitless the whole time, which made it even harder.

Not being from the navy, I was at a disadvantage in some ways, as everyone else seemed to have known each other for years. But on the plus side my five years in the army meant the physical exercises seemed to come easier to me than to most of the navy lads.

A couple of them couldn't believe it when I turned up to do the physical stuff in a pair of battered old basketball boots instead of the fancy trainers they all wore, and their eyes nearly popped out of their heads when I outswam the lot of them. They seemed to hurt themselves more too. One really good mate I made on CDAT, Mark Hudson, or Huddo, had a blister covering the entire sole of his foot but he soldiered on regardless and made it through. Other lads taped up every individual toe and one even taped up his whole ball bag. Thanks to years of pack marching, I didn't get a single blister or even need a Band Aid. It helped too that in the army you learned to snatch sleep at any spare moment you could; you use sleep as a weapon in your armoury. So whenever I wasn't being tested, I slept, which really helped me preserve my energy. Riding the canoe into shore with the tide, I went to sleep. Ten minutes to eat? I ate in two and slept the rest. During the basic course, I even tied myself to a rock and went to sleep underwater. What can I say? Soldiers just know how to make the most of their spare time. And, however much I hurt, however tired I was, I was determined to keep going. I didn't want to go back to the army, I wanted to be a clearance diver. I wanted to make a new life for myself.

By the time we finally finished the course there were only ten of us still standing. In the last ten days we'd each run or forced-marched around 95 kilometres, finned 23 kilometres, carried a stretcher, pack or canoe over 28 kilometres and paddled 67 kilometres – and all on only 51 hours sleep. One by one we were each called into an interview to find out if we'd made the grade. When it was my turn, they sat me down, told me I'd got an A pass and started to say really nice things about me. I was amazed and my eyes started welling up. They said I'd been accepted, and well done. As I got up to walk out, I was so emotional that they were all laughing.

'Congratulations!' one of them said. 'Come here and give us a handshake.' I shook all their hands then walked out, beaming from ear to ear. I felt I was finally on my way to being one of those guys who others look up to and respect. It was the greatest feeling of my life.

# 14

## A GROWN-UP BOYS' ADVENTURE CLUB

The doctor was becoming agitated.

'Look,' he was saying, 'you've got to have surgery.' I shook my head.

'No,' I said. 'No way.' There was absolutely no way I was going to agree to have surgery if I couldn't then go on the final course to become accepted as a clearance diver.

It had been only two months since I'd passed CDAT, and now I was seeing my dream of a new career disintegrate before my very eyes. I'd been sent from CDAT to the navy's base and training establishment *HMAS Cerberus* on Victoria's Mornington Peninsula, back near where I'd started my life, to complete the Royal Australian Navy Staff Acquaint Course. For me and the airforce guy, who'd also got through CDAT, it was a five-week catch-up course about the navy – basically a shortened form of basic navy training, teaching us about the structure of the service, and its rules and regulations. It was like, *Quick, that's a submarine, this is a ship, that's a boat, don't shoot that guy and away you go.*

The course was dead boring so pretty much all we did was train up ready for the big 33-week basic clearance divers course ahead. Neither of us could wait for it to start. At the end of it we'd be qualified clearance divers, part of an elite service right at the forefront of the defence forces. It felt like yet another new beginning, but this time one that held so much promise.

Six weeks before it was due to start, however, I noticed a lump in my groin. I tried to ignore it at first, and almost managed to convince myself it was just a big vein, but it seemed to be growing. When I finally went in to see the doctor, he had bad news: it was an inguinal hernia, when tissue pushes out through a weak spot in the groin muscle. It had been aggravated by all the physical training I was doing and needed to be operated on. When I told the doc I had to start a new course in a month, he was unsympathetic.

'No, you won't be able to do that,' he said. 'It's not possible.'

I dug in my heels. He started to become angry, saying that my intestines would push through my abdominal wall, and the condition would only get worse with all the training and lifting of heavy objects. I was unmoved. If I couldn't go on the course, I wouldn't be treated. Eventually, he gave up and phoned the dive school. They agreed that if I had the surgery, I could still do the course four weeks later.

'Okay!' I said, on being told the news. 'Let's do it.'

An hour after the surgery I woke up feeling on top of the

world – and hungry. I got out of bed and said I was going for a walk to find some food. The nurses looked at me in disbelief.

'Are you trying to set a world record or something?' one of them asked. 'Get back into bed and we'll bring you something to eat.'

The next day I leapt out of bed again . . . and this time the pain in my abdomen was so bad that I passed out. The nurses scooped me up and manhandled me back to bed. The day before, it seemed, I'd still had enough drugs in my system to think I was invincible. But now the pain had kicked in and I couldn't even move. Slowly, over the next few hours, the pain gradually subsided and I did get up and walk, but it hurt like hell. I also noticed I was walking with a limp. For the first time I started to worry that I really wouldn't be well enough to complete the diving course.

The following morning I decided drastic action was needed to get myself back to normal in time for the course. After two days in hospital I checked myself out. As I was leaving, the doctor came racing after me to ask me what was going on. I explained that since I knew my own body well, I'd rather look after my recovery at home. I felt I'd get better much more quickly under my own steam in the comfort of home rather than in the hospital. He was dubious but that afternoon I flew to Sydney, where I was living in the Shire, in the south, and took charge of my own rehabilitation. In truth all I was supposed to do was rest and I knew I'd be much better off doing that at home than in a hospital bed.

Some three weeks later I made it to the course at *HMAS Penguin* on the Sydney Harbour foreshore of Hunter Bay on the city's North Shore, doing PT, running and lifting light weights. If it came to hauling anything heavy, I tried but it just hurt too much and the others helped me out. Luckily, most of the first stage of the course was easy stuff, like learning how to be in charge of the boat as the coxswain, particularly steering and navigation, and learning to drive the dive launch and jet boat, and basic demolitions. I was able to give my body enough time to recover.

As I grew stronger I was able to join in with all the physical activity. I loved that as much as I'd always done and, since we were so competitive and we'd try to out-run, out-swim and out-chin-up each other, I enjoyed it even more. I was able to help the navy boys with their military skills too. When a clearance diver enters enemy territory to clear a beach, he still has to fight, shoot, dig gun pits and get the enemy out of their pit.

And I found I loved the boats. The first time I ever drove one was at the helm of a jet boat out past the heads of the harbour, leaping off the waves, bouncing up and down, racing against the others.

There were things that were hard, and which took me a while to catch on to. I wasn't the sharpest tool in the box. You forget stuff, you're tired. One time on the demolitions part of the course – learning how to use a variety of different explosive techniques and tools – I was connecting a detonator to a safety fuse and I didn't close the metal container that I took the fuse out of. That's a stupid mistake: a signal could have set off another detonator in the box. You also have to learn to cut plastic explosives correctly so you don't get any crumbs on your clothes. It's all about being extremely well-trained, taking the utmost care and using split-second timing. Everything clearance divers do is inherently dangerous, like demolitions and boarding ships and diving, and safety is paramount. But by the same token it's a job that's great fun – getting pumped with physical exercise and then going out driving fast and blowing stuff up. At times it's just like being in a grown-up boys' adventure club.

As for the dive training, that was a revelation. While I had the advantage of always feeling at home in the water, diving was a whole new ball game. I had to learn how to operate the recompression chambers, which allow the diver to recover after a deep or long dive to avoid decompression illness, 'the bends', when dangerous gas bubbles form inside the body and aren't given time to dissipate when the diver comes back up. It's for that reason that, when you ascend, you have to have a number of stops along the way to allow your body to adjust from the pressure of the water deeper down.

Then I had to study deep-air diving, and learn how to use protective dive helmets, which are positively pressurised with air from the surface so that water doesn't flood them, and provide air for breathing and a microphone for communication with other divers and the surface. I was also instructed on how to wear non-contaminable suits or 'dry bags', which are used when the water is extremely cold or contaminated with chemicals. I was taught how to lay an underwater grid for searching too, where tensioned lines are laid below the surface of the water in a rigorous pattern, along a designated bearing. Divers then swim along those lines, searching the area for mines with a sonar device. They search in a sweep that's both methodical and thorough, incorporating overlapping arcs. It means, hopefully, that nothing will ever be missed. Divers communicate with others at the surface via a series of coded tugs on their line: either a pull, which is a steady single heave on the line; or a bell, a sharp quick tug. When they're finished one search, the grid can be wound back onto reels and moved to sweep the next area. It's a very slow process but there's constant work being done to develop quicker, more thorough and accurate ways of conducting such searches.

Later I went on to work with tools for underwater battle-damage repair, where I learned how to use underwater chainsaws and drills, and how to weld under water. That involves using a Broco Ultrathermic gun with a cutting rod temperature of over 5000°C, which will slice through, or melt, almost anything, including steel, cast iron, brass and concrete. When you're working, you've got two lines: one powering the tool and the other shooting oxygen through a nozzle to allow it to burn. The real danger is getting between the gun and the job and becoming part of the circuit, and that can really, really hurt. I found that out through bitter experience when one day the sea current pushed me in between and . . . *BANG!* I suffered a huge electric shock. It's a mistake you only make once. After a few seconds to get my bearings, I picked the welding gun back up and kept going, just like you'd have to in a real situation.

One of the hardest phases of the course was maritime tactical operations, where you learn how to be an attack and reconnaissance swimmer with a rifle on your back, a pistol on your leg and a backpack full of explosives, using an oxygen re-breather set and following directions underwater, with a compass board and a depth gauge. It's enjoyable, but it's very intense.

The underwater demolitions were a great part of the training.

For that, you went to Shoalwater Bay off the coast of central Queensland near Rockhampton, where the navy has its own little spot, Triangular Island, with a nice beach on one side, but mud-flats on the other. Our luggage was pretty heavy – 32 tonnes of bombs and explosives, two semitrailers' full, all of which we had to offload from the boat to the island by hand. Our brief was to place bombs in specific locations. We were given a map reference and ended up dragging four 500-pound bombs and six 125-kilogram mine-disposable charges a kilometre out over the mudflats, wading through a mire of knee-deep mud. It was great fun but extremely hard work and most days we were covered head to toe in mud.

For the duration of the exercises, we lived on the island in tents, with no showers and just the ocean to bathe in. When the tide came in over the mudflats, the water turned dark, a murky pond so thick with mud that once submerged, divers had to do everything by feel. That was fun too. By far the worst part of the whole trip was burning the shitters. We'd make toilets out of 44-gallon drums and then the person on shit duty that day had to pour diesel into them, set them alight and stir until there was nothing left. Everyone got a turn. Apart from the odd moment like that, I was truly having the time of my life. I'd found something I loved, and wanted to give it 110 per cent.

### Dalla

Once Paul found something he was really interested in, he would always be the kind of person to put in that extra bit to achieve his goal. He also thrives on competition, mainly with himself, I think. The fact he made it as a clearance diver is testament to that determination. But what he also has is self-belief and a forward approach to life. The focused training that the army and navy deliver really brought that out in him, and pushed it to the fore. Some people like Paul have just got it all along, waiting, but it might take a while to realise it. And as soon as he'd discovered it, he just knew how to use it.

Once we'd completed the basic clearance divers course, a few people from different navy branches – called 'rates' – had to return to *HMAS Cerberus* for small-arms training. To me that seemed crazy – sending an ex-paratrooper to go and learn how to shoot. But I ended up pretty much doing the instructing since none of the others had ever learnt. As soon as word went round that I was teaching my colleagues how to shoot, a leading seaman came down to check me out. He asked me to go through my weapons drill and my safety check, which I did quickly and efficiently. He just stood staring.

'I've never seen anyone do that so fast before,' he said finally. I was left alone to get on with it after that.

Finally, we had to do the last part of the course on seamanship – how to tie knots, fire-fighting and survival at sea. By then we were wearing our blue uniforms with our clearance divers' badges sewn on the shirts, until some officer noticed and we were ordered to unstitch our badges until we'd finished the seamanship course. We were understandably pissed off as we'd just spent the better half of a year earning those patches. We told him that if he wanted them, he'd have to come and take them off us himself. He didn't.

One of my most vivid memories from that course was getting

gassed. It seemed as though no matter which branch of the services I chose, they all liked to gas me, just so I'd know what it felt like. In the army I'd been sprayed with OC spray, a more condensed form of pepper spray, which feels like rubbing deep heat into your eyeballs and then setting your face on fire. I was glad I wasn't having to go through that again. This time I was dressed in lead-lined clothes, given a gas mask, and led into a little room. They fed in CS gas – tear gas – and I had to take off the mask and say my name, rank and date of birth before I could put it back on. Having been through the same exercise before in the army, I took great delight in seeing the frightened faces of navy recruits going through it for the first time. Usually, before you're even halfway through your name, you can't breathe, your nose starts running, your eyes are watering, you're coughing and spluttering and your skin starts burning.

In short, gassing tends to hurt, and it can hurt a fucking lot. But when you're under attack in a war zone, the last thing you need is to fall apart. Getting us used to pain, and letting us know what to expect when it hit, was all part of the training.

# 15

## SHARK BAIT

It was during one of those deep dives on the training course that I
had to really confront my fear of sharks. I think it had been getting
worse since I was a kid. As I got older, and TV shows about sharks
became more bloody and explicit, I would never go out surfing
by myself, *ever*. I'd always take one or two people out with me so
we could keep an eye on each other, help each other out if need
be, and, of course, it was always a lot more fun to have mates
around. At the very least, I'd joke, having buddies there would
cut down the chances of an attack on me by at least 50 per cent.

Now I was spending more time in the water, I found I was
steadily becoming more nervous about the idea of sharks. One day,
after a couple of weeks of diving training, I was 1 or 2 kilometres
outside the heads of Sydney Harbour, going down deep. My buddy
diver found he couldn't clear his ears and, without being able to

equalise the pressure between his middle ear and the outside, risked bursting an eardrum if he went lower, so was ordered back up to the surface. I, on the other hand, was told to carry on. At the prospect of diving alone, my heart sank to the bottom of the ocean below me. I instantly started to imagine company: a school of shadowy sentinels circling me.

I carried on descending, down, down, deeper and down. At 54 metres I stopped at the concrete block called a 'shot', which marked the lowest point I was diving to. From there I could glimpse the sand at the bottom of the ocean. Finally, after a tense few minutes, I got the signal to go back up, and started my ascent. On the way I had to do a five-minute decompression stop at 9 metres. Then it hit me: I was here, alone, in the big bad ocean, sitting on the end of a rope like a little worm on a hook, just waiting for a feeding shark. The water was quite misty and I could see only 4 metres in any direction. Beyond that there could be anything lurking. My mind started playing tricks on me and my imagination ran riot. I saw great white sharks swimming all around me, getting ready to pounce on their tasty snack. I couldn't get up to the surface fast enough. The next stop I was forced to make at 3 metres felt like it lasted forever.

I had a similar experience near the end of that course, during the part where you practise swimming as if you're going to attack an enemy ship. Laden with weapons and explosives, concentrating on directions and trying to swim at exactly the right depth for hours was both physically and psychologically draining. At the point of absolute exhaustion I started seeing shadows. I could have sworn I saw those great whites circling round again.

As a clearance diver I hadn't really received any instruction about dealing with sharks. At dive briefs, we'd just be told that if we encountered a dangerous marine animal to 'exercise caution'. That's pretty bloody obvious, really.

One day, during training, I happened to mention my fear of sharks to some of the boys. That was a huge mistake. I'm sure some of them were afraid as well, but they just never mentioned it. Now I'd made myself a target. Any time there was a shark attack somewhere in the world one of the boys would bring in a newspaper clipping or a printed-out online article. If anyone stumbled across a good photo of a great white, they'd pin it up on my locker or on the wall close to where I worked. Whenever we went out for diving exercises or underwater-demolitions training at the island in Shoalwater Bay, they'd regale me with stories about 5-metre tiger sharks seen floating in the waters nearby. For them, it was a huge joke, but I'm sure there was also an element of bravado in it. Laughing about it was a great way of dealing with their own fears.

But, to be serious, anyone regularly in the water, like us clearance divers, was more at risk from sharks now than at any other time in history. Worldwide, according to statistics from the International Shark Attack File, the number of shark attacks was climbing steadily, from just 80 across the globe in the 1930s to 650 in the nine years from 2000 – although admittedly there were not as many figures collected in the '30s, the population was a lot smaller and fewer people used the water for recreation. In Australia, a country with the dubious honour of sitting second on the world league table for shark attacks, behind only the USA, the annual figure had risen substantially, especially over recent years. In 1999, for example, there was only one shark attack. In 2006, the year I finished my diver training, that had risen to seven, including one that had proved fatal. In 2007 that leapt to thirteen.

The jump in the number of shark attacks is mostly a result of there being far more sharks close to the Australian coast and in its waterways. In Sydney Harbour alone there have been 30 shark attacks since 1791 – despite beaches later being netted – with the last fatal shark attack back in 1963 when the actress Marcia Hathaway was taken in shallow waters at Sugarloaf Bay. But in 2002 a kayaker was knocked into the water by a bull shark in the Parramatta River and had to be rescued by fishermen as he clung to a buoy. Two months later a 3-metre bull shark was hooked by fishermen at Rushcutters Bay. Now there were regular reports of shark spottings in the harbour, and many felt it was only a matter of time until the next attack. With much of the industry that used to pollute the harbour having disappeared over the previous ten years, sewage and storm run-off being reduced and a ban on commercial fishing being enforced, the water is a great deal cleaner and there are a lot more fish around to attract sharks. Some experts say that global warming is also bringing them closer to shore to feed because of changes in the water temperature altering fish migratory patterns and leading to shortages of food in sharks' usual feeding grounds.

I've thought a lot over the years about my relationship with sharks. I've come to the conclusion that it's not the sharks themselves that are the issue; I think it's more the fear of being eaten alive. I've swum many times with sharks and, although they're not exactly cute and cuddly, they've always seemed calm and far less likely to attack me than a cranky dog.

It's easy to say that there's a better chance of being struck by lightning than of being attacked by a shark – but try telling that to someone who's been hit by lightning. At the end of the day, though, you have to be realistic. If you play in the shark's domain then you always risk suffering the consequences.

It's not that I never came up against sharks in my career as a clearance diver. I spent a lot of time working in Jervis Bay on NSW's south coast with Clearance Diving Team One. One time when we were at the end of our exercise, Huddo, my mate from the course, and I were out on one of the jet boats retrieving some leftover lines from a clandestine beach survey grid. Huddo jumped into the water and from the boat, I could hear laughter coming out of his snorkel.

'What's so funny, giggles?' I called down to him.

He surfaced, took the snorkel out of his mouth and said, 'I can't pull the line up. I think there's a shark on it!' It was just so unexpected, he couldn't stop laughing.

Without even thinking about it, I said I'd get in there and have a look, so I threw on my mask and fins, strapped a knife to my leg and jumped in. With Huddo holding the line, I dove down to have a look. He was right – there was a metre-long shark, and not a very happy-looking one, with the line wrapped in a figure eight through its gills and around its fins. It had probably been trapped there most of the night. I seized its tail in one hand, surfaced, flicked it over on its back, and told Huddo to cut the line. The shark, a wobbegong, I thought, was looking straight at Huddo at this stage, maybe blaming him for the mess it was in.

I tried to unwrap it from the line while holding its body still. Huddo cut extremely carefully as wobbegongs are remarkably flexible and can do a full turn to bite a hand holding them by the tail. When the line was cut, I flipped the shark over but its head ended up right by Huddo's head. At that point it tried to take a bite out of his face. I pulled it away and finally managed to get it loose. Then I did a 180-degree turn and pushed the cranky shark into the crystal-clear bay and watched it swim off. But it didn't seem to want to go far, and just kept swimming around us as we finished the job we'd started.

Wobbegongs are a species of bottom-feeding carpet shark that don't generally attack humans unless they're provoked. They do have a severe bite, however, and can do a lot of damage as they often don't like to let go. Pleased that this one was free and we were still intact, I got out of the water and back in the boat with a smile on my face. We cranked up the engine and began our return leg to base. The sun was pulsing bright on the water of the bay as we slid across its surface. I looked back at Huddo over my shoulder and grinned.

'Why would you ever want to do anything else?' I asked.

It was a strange little encounter with that shark, and a good one, on reflection. Huddo had been amazed at me keeping my cool – he was one of the main players in the game to torment me about sharks – and he'd had a lucky escape from having his face chomped. Given I'd always been so nervous of sharks, I suppose it sounds strange that I was the one to go straight into the water to confront this one. But that was part of my job, and it was a job I loved more than anything else. I wasn't prepared to let anything, even my own fear of sharks, stop me from doing that job to the best of my ability.

If we'd been diving at night, perhaps that shark would have caused us a bit of trouble. Maybe we'd had a lucky escape . . . or maybe it had. But whoever had come off best, I hoped the close call with that shark would mean it would be a long time before I came across another.

# 16

## I'M FROM THE ARMY; I HAVE NO IDEA

Why does everyone in the navy hate divers?

It's something that confused me no end in my first years with the clearance divers. Whenever our divers play rugby against the New Zealand divers, the Aussie fleet barrack for the Kiwis. We're often the butt of snide remarks and jokes about divers' lifestyles, since we're allowed a lot more freedom than other members of the navy. There's occasionally even a bit of real hostility.

I started asking around. The first answer I got didn't help much. 'Probably a diver rooted their missus,' suggested someone. But then a real trend emerged: 'It's because they're jealous, that's why.' And, really, why wouldn't they be? You spend a lot of your time in Speedos, driving around in fast boats and blowing up stuff. The rest of the time you're in army camouflage instead of the regular navy blue or grey overalls – although we've since been put back into navy blues. You're given liberties and freedoms that others aren't: you're paid more, you get longer holidays, you work separately from the rest of the navy, and you're a small team so you know everyone and the camaraderie is awesome. And, to top it all off, you're pretty popular with women too. In short, life just doesn't get much better.

Graduating from the course in April 2006 to become a fully fledged member of the branch was one of my proudest days. I knew that at times there might be tough jobs to do, but I'd always loved a challenge. No one ever wants a war but if one came along, I'd be completely prepared for anything that might be thrown at me. I was ready and waiting.

I felt, at that point, I had it all: a job I absolutely loved, a beautiful girl, Kim, I'd just started seeing, a new motorbike that was my pride and joy – a big black V twin Italian sports bike, an Aprilia RSV 1000R – and I'd just rediscovered surfing, which was fast becoming a real passion. I also had a new bunch of mates, who'd given me the nickname 'DG' after my surname but also short, they said, for 'Dangerous Goods'. After an often miserable childhood and the wild days of my youth, the struggle to adapt to the discipline of the army and then the long and gruelling selection process to get into the clearance divers, I finally felt I'd found my place in life.

My first posting was to underwater battle-damage repair at Australian Clearance Diving Team One at *HMAS Waterhen* in Sydney's Waverton, the navy's parent establishment for the team as well as Australia's Mine Countermeasures Force. The mine hunter coastal (MHC) ships were berthed there and we assisted with any maintenance that was asked of us. The rest of the time I carried out maintenance work on other ships, went diving, worked out and enjoyed the free time.

The first trip out to sea came early. Huddo, had been posted aboard an MHC, *HMAS Diamantina*, going up to Darwin and then around Southeast Asia. A few days after he'd set sail, I was asked if I'd like to go up to take the place of a diver who'd been sent home. Thinking I'd be joining Huddo on an adventure, I readily agreed. It was only later that I discovered *he* was the one who'd been sent back after going ashore at port in Darwin, 'falling in love' with a girl and not turning up for duty the next day when the ship sailed. But it was a great trip anyway, and I spent two months sailing up through the South China Sea and the Malacca Strait and then around Malaysia, Thailand, Indonesia and Singapore, with a couple of dives along the way. Most nights we had to man pirate-watches, armed with loaded automatic rifles. We also conducted regular manoeuvring drills with our sister ship, *HMAS Houn*, with quite a few man-overboard using a dummy. I was so keen I volunteered to do the majority of rescues, leaping from the side of the ship into a sea sometimes 5000 metres deep. I also ran into my brother Sean, who I hadn't seen in two years, in Singapore. He was en route to a defence shooting competition in the UK and had bumped into a few lads off the ship hitting the tins at a Singapore bar. It was great to catch up.

Being on that little ship was a whole new experience, including sleeping on a top bunk with such a tiny space between me and the ceiling. Half the time I had a divot in my head from where I kept hitting it. In addition my feet would constantly be up against the wall and every time I rolled over, half my body would dangle out of the bed. But the navy guys were used to it; it's what they do. But that, and the constant watches and cleaning stations, nearly killed me. I was a highly trained clearance diver doing a boat-swain's job, and when you compare our nine-month basic course to the eight-week one they do, you can imagine my frustration at sea time aboard a mine hunter. When we finally docked back in Darwin, I asked the captain if I could fly back to the dive team in Sydney. To my surprise, he was fine about it.

Always pleased to be given the chance to go away and do my job, I got another trip soon after, an exercise called 'Bersama Lima' in the South China Sea and on the Malaysian peninsula, an annual five-power naval, ground and airforce exercise with New Zealand, the UK, Singapore and Malaysia. I was posted to the mine counter-measures element and was part of the team clearing a bay of inert mines, which in reality was the tiny vol-canic jungle-covered Tioman Island off the Malaysian coast. It was an interesting experience and the time we had off was always an adventure. We were the only ones from the Australian force staying onshore, while all the other 'fleeties' just came on land for a day-long sports carnival – and they weren't allowed to drink. In contrast, outside of training, we were allowed to drink beer and go to the resort on the other side of the island, where we would drink cocktails in the pool . . . Yeah, maybe it's no wonder they hate us.

We also had a bit to do with US Navy divers from their Mobile Underwater Diving Salvage Unit up in Gladstone in Queensland. We did some diving on wrecks and diving with pressurised hel-mets as part of a joint exercise, acquainting each with the other's procedures and equipment. It was fun, afterwards, hanging out together. Another memorable experience was taking part, with other navy personnel, in 'The ultimate endurance challenge', the Australian Three Peaks Race, which involved three sailing legs and 135 kilometres' worth of running up three of Tasmania's biggest mountains. Only five of us took part in the running – the rest were happy sailing.

Of course, it wasn't all fun and games. We worked hard and our hours could be long. We started at 7 a.m. and could sometimes work till 2 a.m. only to be back at work again at 7 a.m. But it was fascinating work. The many different roles meant that no two days were ever the same; every one of them brought a new challenge and a different adventure. I also liked the mateship, I loved the freedom and I really enjoyed all the physical activity. We had an hour every single morning dedicated to fitness, when you could swim, run, play tennis, weight-train – anything. It's important to maintain your fitness as a clearance diver not only for the work but also for the diving. The leaner you are, the less nitrogen you absorb, as it tends to accumulate more in fat, so the easier it is to dispel it without risking decompression sickness.

In between the hard work we always managed a few laughs. At first I had to get used to navy ways, and a lot of their protocols were lost on me. One day on a ship I was on duty on the gangway at port in Singapore. When a bunch of officers came on board, I was supposed to stand to attention, salute them, announce their arrival on the ship's piping system, their PA service, and so on. Instead, I sat on my chair, feet up on the rail, my sleeves rolled up, reading *FHM* magazine, feeling terribly hung-over from the night before. As each one stepped aboard, I greeted them with a casual, 'G'day, sir.' But no one complained. They just told each other, 'He's from the army. He doesn't know what he's meant to do.'

It became a well-worn excuse for my mistakes. A ship's piping system is for communicating official messages to the whole ship and, unknown to me at the time, the announcements have to be worded in a particular way, in a tone that's strictly directed. While on duty on the gangway, I felt thirsty. So I picked up the piping system phone and said, 'This is DG on the gangway. Can someone get me a drink?' and hung up. Then I had a sudden thought and picked it up again. 'Make that an apple juice.' It was apparently the first time anyone had done that, and people were either shocked or wetting themselves that I'd been using the system as my own personal phone, as if I were ordering room service. I didn't know; I was from the army.

Another time I was driving the ship at 2 a.m. in the South China Sea when I was given a particular task to do on the ship's control system. I had no idea how to do it but felt sure I could figure it out. We clearance divers usually operate out of smaller boats with few technical controls and here I was driving a multi-million-dollar warship with a major weapons system. The trouble is, because we're divers, people trust us.

No sooner had I started pressing buttons, than the alarm *WOO! WOO! WOO!* started booming around the ship. I thought, *Oh shit!* and tried to stop it. But I was out of the menu screen, and had to go back through the sub-menus, and it took me ages. By then the whole ship thought we had a real emergency and everyone had leapt from their beds and was running around everywhere.

Naturally, I apologised, but being able to say, 'I'm an ex-grunt; I didn't know' saved me yet again. It was like having a Teflon coating somehow.

Yet as divers, we did do our fair share of good PR for the navy. Off-duty, you can always spot a clearance diver: he's the one insisting he's a dolphin trainer, or that he works putting stickers on apples or as a Lego technician. But at work, you give it everything. Huddo and I were sent to Geelong in Victoria to the Avalon Airshow and then to Canberra to do weekend clearance-diver displays at events. We took weapons, underwater chainsaws, diving helmets and our new 20 000-litre dive tank to show all the gear to the visitors at our tent. Sometimes we did underwater demonstrations in the tank too, playing noughts and crosses from inside on the Perspex with kids, or kissing the glass for the girls.

In Canberra we went out that Friday night, got separated and partied late. The next morning we received furious calls from the chief, asking where the fuck we were. I dragged myself out of the bed of a woman I'd hooked up with, and we each arrived late from the different places we'd spent the night. I was relieved when I was able to get away up in a chopper and do a drop-down into Lake Burley Griffin for the crowd. It was the perfect antidote to a big night.

We proved a real hit with the public. We'd lay out all the diving gear, which was pretty impressive, but everyone always made a beeline for the weapons. In Canberra one guy came on the hour, every hour, each day to look at the guns, and pick them up to see what they felt like. I hate to think what must have been going through his mind. The kids loved the guns best as well, especially when we brought out the M4 carbine, which replaced the old assault rifle, and added on all the special attachments, like the night-vision sight, the night-aiming device, the silencer, torch and front grip. At the start the gun weighed 4 kilograms but by the end it was about 12 kilograms, more than a machine-gun. None of the kids could even pick it up. It was amazing, though, how well they knew all the moving parts of guns – I guess through TV shows – and how they would flock around. It was also incredible how many women fawned over us. Being a clearance diver seems sometimes to prove a powerful aphrodisiac. Well, we like to think so anyway.

In my personal life I wasn't doing too badly with women. Since getting stronger, fitter and more confident in the defence forces, I'd had a lot of girlfriends, but had recently got together with a girl called Kim, the best friend of Dalla's girlfriend, Kylie. We first met at a friend's bogan fancy-dress party. It wasn't instant attraction – I was wearing a singlet, trackies, thongs and big fake teeth, while she wore a moustache and a false beer belly – but we soon discovered we had a lot in common. We had a similar sense of humour and she was really into fitness as well. I think she was a bit nervous about getting involved at first: she said she'd been warned off me and told I was trouble, and a bit of a commitment-phobe. Her informers were right there. I wasn't in any hurry to settle down and was still seeing a couple of other girls. I didn't want to get serious, as I went away so often, and I was hoping to go away again in March 2009 for four months on an exchange program to England. But we just liked hanging out together. I felt comfortable with her.

I wrote Kimmy a couple of training programs for the gym and

we'd often meet up afterwards, have a run on the sand together at Bondi, where I rented a unit, and then she'd come back to my place for dinner. I liked cooking and I introduced her to kangaroo in my own take on spaghetti bolognese, spaghetti bolo-roo. She also loved my bike and the sense of complete freedom it brought. By this stage she was staying at my place nearly every weekend, in what she called 'Degelderathons'. But a lot of my time and energy were always taken up with work.

As a clearance diver you're on call nearly all the time, since any bombs found near water are your responsibility as well as any ships that become damaged or need attention, and this can happen at any time. Another big part of our work is helping test new equipment and systems for a war scenario or as part of counter-terrorism exercises. One day in February 2009 when I was working in mine counter-measures, a group of us was taken into a briefing room and told about new sonar devices that were being built both here and overseas to detect enemy divers in the water. The next stage was to test them to see if they would protect our ships, naval bases and Australian ports. We were asked if we'd take part in a trial. We all readily agreed – until we were told we'd have to sign a waiver beforehand.

That came as a complete surprise, and continues to this day to be a mystery. It was the first time we'd ever been asked to sign a waiver for any of our work, and pretty much everyone said no. In our jobs we were asked to do plenty of dangerous, life-threatening jobs, so why the waiver all of a sudden? It didn't make sense. Were the sonars likely to affect us in some way? The blokes in charge started going through a mountain of theory and explaining the physics of the devices to try to allay our fears. Some of the guys finally said all right, but others still said no way. I was in the second group. I felt if I signed the waiver, I'd basically be giving up all my rights to the navy's duty of care.

But then again I did have that application in the system to go to the UK on exchange, and I worried that might somehow be affected.

It was only later I found out that the waiver was a requirement when working on an exercise in conjunction with the Defence, Science and Technology Organisation (DSTO), which is the government's agency that handles the science of national security. But back then it had me stumped. I did think, though, I would be letting my chief down if I continued to refuse. And if I didn't do it, someone else would have to. So I thought, *Hell! I might as well man up*. I said I'd do it.

The group of us who'd agreed were told to report for duty the next day at Garden Island, the navy port on Sydney harbour for its major fleet on the east coast of Australia, at 6 a.m. sharp. That evening I went to the gym with Kim and then told her I'd go home alone and get to bed early. I had to be up at 4 a.m. the next day for the exercise, and I wanted to make sure I was ready for whatever the day might bring.

# PART THREE

# OVERCOME

# 17

## NO TIME FOR FEAR

The sun had just risen when I roared up on my motorbike at 6 a.m. on Wednesday, 11 February 2009 for Exercise Kondari – the sonar tests at Sydney's naval base on Garden Island. It had been raining the night before and it was a damp, cloudy morning, overcast and gloomy with a bit of a chill in the air. The water was pretty calm but murky. Nobody took much notice of that, though. There was too much happening on the wharf.

Already there was quite a crowd there: the other clearance divers taking part in the exercise that day, a support crew, our supervisor, Patto – Lane Patterson – a number of people from the navy, officials from the Department of Defence's Defence Science and Technology Organisation, some police divers and representatives of the various companies whose equipment we were testing. They'd set it all up both on the bow of the ship *HMAS Success*, tied up alongside the wharf, and on the wharf itself, together with a video camera to record everything that went on.

One of my fellow divers, a new guy called Arthur McLachlin – Lachy – jumped in the water from the Zodiac, the black rubber dinghy we used as the safety boat, and swam a few laps between where we were, near Fort Denison, and the supply ship *HMAS Success* about 100 metres away while everyone trained the sonars on him. It was pretty boring as jobs go; he was just swimming back and forth, back and forth. After a while of watching him, I pulled him out of the water and told him I'd finish it off. I fancied a swim and paddling up and down the water of Sydney Harbour was just another cruisy day in one of the most beautiful spots in the country. I didn't see doing Lachy a good turn as much of a hardship. Famous last words.

I slipped over the side into the water and had just started swimming his route out towards the bow of the ship when it happened. I was on my back in my regulation navy anti-stinger wetsuit kicking my legs, about 50 metres from the wharf, wondering idly whether in a shark attack it'd be better to have your arms crossed over your chest or down in the water. There'd already been a record five attacks in Australia over the previous several weeks – although not one in the harbour for a decade – and the newspapers were full of them. I then looked over my left shoulder to make sure I was heading in the right direction. I hadn't even begun to turn back when I felt an almighty whack on the leg. I didn't think too much of it at first. It didn't hurt. I just thought it was strange, that I must have swum into a buoy or a log or maybe a boat I hadn't heard had run into me.

Half a second later I turned over, looked down to check my leg and saw the huge grey head of a bull shark, one of nature's most aggressive man-eaters, known as 'the pit bull of the sea'. What's more I could see the upper row of its teeth across my leg. Its lip was pulled back – when sharks attack, their jaws protrude – and its mouth looked fucking enormous. I could see everything: the teeth in my leg, its gums and one of its glittering black eyes. It took an instant to compute. I remember thinking, *What's going on? That's not meant to be there!*

We must have stared at each other for about three seconds but as soon as I recovered from the shock and realised what I was looking at, I started fighting for my life. I guess the good thing about having that long-time dread of sharks was that I was wary every time I got into the water, constantly ready for anything going wrong. It was a combination of my instincts and all my years of training.

Up to that point, I thought the shark had just come up for a bite, grabbed me and was waiting to see what would happen next. Usually, we swim in teams, which puts off the sharks as they don't like attacking anything that's likely to put up a fight. Finding me alone probably felt like a stroke of luck, but it wasn't yet sure if I'd be something it could eat. I started moving and tried to lift my right arm to jab it in the eye, knowing that would be its softest, most vulnerable part. But I couldn't seem to move my arm. It was pinned down by my side – I hadn't realised my hand was also in its mouth. I tried to stab it in the eyeball with my other hand. I reached as far as I could, but I was still 15 centimetres away. Instead, I tried to push its nose, but my hand just slid off it. It was like pushing on a slippery concrete wall. When that didn't work, I pulled back my left arm and punched the shark as hard as I could on the nose. It didn't make much difference. The fish was about 3 metres long, probably weighed 200–300 kilos and was like one big muscle. Compared to that, I was a tiny little shred of flesh, a mere morsel in its mouth. There was nothing to hold on to, I couldn't anchor myself. I realised with a sickening feeling that I was completely at its mercy.

After I'd punched it in the head, it must have come to the conclusion I was edible because then it started shaking me like a dog would a rag doll, trying to get away with whatever was in its mouth. Bull sharks impale prey with their lower teeth and use their upper teeth to carve flesh, like a saw, and that's when the pain kicked in and I started yelling. But I didn't get to yell for long. Still holding onto my leg, the shark pulled me down under the water, continuing to shake me. After a few seconds we came back up and I gulped for breath. Almost immediately, I was under again and I saw my fin kick up in the air from the force, and the shark's tail flopping around out past my leg. I remember thinking what a big beast it was.

The second time I went under I could only see bubbles in front of my face. I no longer felt any pain. I couldn't do anything. I was totally helpless. Everything was quiet. There was just a deep silence. And then, just as suddenly, the shark was gone. I was free. I bobbed up to the surface and knew I had to get out of the water as soon as I could. There must be more sharks around, and it wouldn't take long for this one to come back and have another go. I started swimming to the safety boat, doing freestyle, until

I looked up and saw my right hand wasn't there.

It was a shock but my training kicked in immediately. Almost automatically I held the stump out of the water – I didn't want to bleed into the water as that might attract more sharks – and tried swimming side-stroke. I didn't know at that point that the shark had torn my hamstring from my right leg and that I was pumping out so much blood, there was a plume of red all around me. I hadn't realised I was actually in a pool of my own blood.

I was swimming and swimming but it felt as if I wasn't moving. I couldn't really feel my right leg. The safety boat looked far away and I thought, *That's it. I'm dead.* There seemed no way I was going to get to the boat before another shark got me. I could see the boat coming towards me and I was still trying to swim as fast as I could, but I was getting nowhere. I thought I was finished. I wasn't giving up, but I felt I had no chance of getting out of that water alive. I was probably only swimming for five or ten seconds, but it felt like forever as I desperately tried to keep my head above the surface with one hand and the one leg that was still working. Then, finally, the boat got to me. I was shouting, 'Quick! Get me the hell out of the water! Get me out!' And I felt the lads grab me and haul me into the boat; I was out of the water in a second. I don't know who spoke, but I just heard this string of swear words, so I knew I must be in a bad way. Next second, I was on my back in the boat and I just remember thinking, *Oh my God, I'm still alive . . .* then I passed out.

The next thing I knew my mate Jeremy Thomas – Thommo – was punching me in the chest. I thought, *What are you doing?* Then I realised what must be going on. I remembered that my hand was missing and I looked to check it hadn't all been a dream. It wasn't; it was gone. My first aid training kicked back in then and I thought, *Okay I've got to stem the bleeding,* so I grabbed my wrist with my left hand and held it above my head. Ryan Dart – Dartie – was working on my leg at the same time, Thommo was talking to me and Lachy was driving the boat back to the wharf. I could feel Dartie tugging at my leg and I wanted to have a look but I knew that if I looked down and saw bone and half my leg missing, it would affect me mentally. I would go into shock and I would die. So I just didn't look, and hoped for the best. I knew my hand was gone but tried not to think about it. I had no time for fear. I knew that if I could stay talking to Thommo, stay breathing and keep my eyes open, I'd live. So that was the goal: to focus on breathing and keeping my eyes open.

That ride to the wharf is all a bit blurry. I'm pretty sure I stayed awake through it all, but I was concentrating on not dying, so I don't really remember it. The boys told me later that they'd had to improvise to get me from the boat up to the wharf, which is high above the water. Someone climbed onto one of the great big fenders that cushion the wharf from the ships and they heaved me up to there, and then on to the wharf. Our supervisor, Patto, who'd seen the whole thing from his vantage point on the ship, thought I was dead. He was wrong. I was still conscious but I wasn't looking around me; I was concentrating on staying alive. I don't remember the pain at that point. I was probably in shock.

An ambulance seemed to turn up in record time and I think I started feeling pain just before I was loaded in. Then the pain became so bad, I was yelling at the paramedics to give me some drugs. That pain grew worse and worse all the way to hospital. One of the paramedics later told a friend of mine, who's also an ambo, that their strict protocol of administering no more than 5 mL of morphine in the first 20 minutes went out the window when they saw the state I was in; they ended up giving me four times that amount in the first five minutes. The pain sort of went away as a result, but I couldn't breathe. Maybe the amount of morphine they gave me had lowered my blood pressure a lot, and I'd lost so much blood that I just didn't have the energy to move. I couldn't lift a finger. I was really struggling to summon the energy to make my chest go up and down. One of the paramedics coached me through it, telling me to take really, really quick shallow breaths and then reserve my energy for the next big breath. That got me through.

At St Vincent's Hospital there was already a theatre set up and the trauma doctors were waiting for me. I was just so lucky. I was wheeled straight from the ambulance into theatre. The drugs had really kicked in by that stage and I was in no pain. I remember lying on my back and seeing the doctor.

'Doc!' I said. 'I'll buy you a case of beer if you save my leg. I've just started surfing and I really don't want to lose my leg!'

Someone asked me if there was anyone I wanted them to contact, and I said to call Kim. I must have been pretty high on the morphine as I was looking around and saying to the nurses, 'Wow! There are some good-looking nurses here!' I think I was trying everything to take my mind away from what had happened. I felt fine at first with all the drugs, but when they started to wear off, and they couldn't give me any more as they'd given me too much the first time, I was screwed.

And then finally someone gave me an anaesthetic and I went to sleep. Peace at last.

### Leading Seaman Clearance Diver Jeremy Thomas (Thommo), Paul's element leader

On the day of the shark attack I was supervising from the Zodiac. Paul's one of the best guys I've had working for me. He's a professional and if there was a difficult or complicated task, Paul was the go-to man. You'd dare him to do a job and he'd do it quicker and faster and better than anyone.

We were out there that day testing sonars to detect enemy divers and I'd just turned my head to talk to the two other guys on the boat, Lachy and Dartie, when we all heard a yell. I turned back to see Paul about 50 metres away with a shark attached to him, with blood and splashing and shouting. I saw the shark's nose and its fin and Paul underneath being launched into the air. They were both on the surface, then they went under for a second, then came back up again. I made the command straightaway to get over there and spoke on our communications system to Lane Patterson on the boat, who was the overall supervisor on the day, to tell him we had a shark attack. From the tone of my voice, he knew we were serious.

As we got closer to Paul, I think the shark was startled by the noise from the boat, the roar of the engine and the vibrations it made underwater, and swam away. Paul's body was submerged in bloody water so it was hard to see how he was. He looked as if he'd been cut in half: his upper body seemed to be at a 90-degree angle with his lower half. I got Lachy to grab his legs, Dartie to grab his midriff and I grabbed his upper body and arms. I was scared if we pulled just part of him up, his body might fall apart under the weight. This way, if his leg did separate from his body, we'd be able to retrieve it as well.

We hauled him into the boat and lay him on his back on the floor. His leg had a great gaping wound, pouring with blood, and what had been his hand was like empty skin, looking like something that'd come out of a meat grinder. Then his eyes rolled back into his head and he fell in and out of consciousness. I realised at that point we were losing him. It was going to be touch and go.

The most important things were to stop the blood flow from the leg and to deal with the shock. There was nothing in the medical kit for injuries this severe, and haemorrhaging this bad, so we used what was around us. We pulled off our T-shirts to plug the gaping hole in his leg, packed it tight and used the strap from a lifejacket to put pressure on the wound and stabilise his leg. When his eyes rolled, I knew I needed to bring him back and keep him conscious. So I gave him a series of short, sharp thumps on the chest to stimulate his heart and make him open his eyes again. He finally opened them and then I focused everything on his eyes and told him to keep looking into my eyes and listening to my voice. I kept reassuring him he'd be okay, he'd be fine, that we were nearly at the wharf, that the ambulance was on its way, but he had to keep his eyes open. At the same time I shielded him from seeing his leg as I felt if he saw it, that wouldn't be good for him.

At that point Paul even managed to crack a few jokes. We

played along with it as best we could as we knew we had to keep him conscious. He said it looked as if he mightn't be riding home to Bondi that night on his bike. He also asked if someone could look after it for him.

When we got to the wharf, the police divers also at the exercise helped us create a chain of arms. We placed Paul's body on top and lifted him the 1.5 metres up onto the pontoon below the wharf. There we gave him oxygen and Patto jumped down from the wharf. I'll never forget his face. He went white. I'm sure he thought Paul was dead. But then he found a piece of line lying on the pontoon and he cut a piece and tourniquetted Paul's leg with it. An ambulance had arrived by then and the paramedics came down on to the pontoon to help too. Some contractors who were working on *HMAS Kuttabul* had seen what was happening and we yelled out to them that we needed bodies to help build a bridge to get Paul up the two or so metres to the wharf. They brought over planks of wood and rails lying around and we built a makeshift bridge for us to walk up carrying Paul, and put him straight into the ambulance. Patto went along to hospital with him.

After it was all over, we just stood there and there was a momentary pause. What the hell just happened?

### Petty Officer Clearance Diver Lane Patterson (Patto), Paul's supervisor

When the shark attacked, I was standing on the bow of the *HMAS Success* watching Paul swim towards us. I'd first met him when he was going through his divers course and always thought he was a good operator – very fit and mentally switched on. He was definitely in the top 20 per cent of divers. I was chatting to the guys when one of them said there's something going on – the boat's speeding over to Paul. Then Thommo's voice came over the headset: 'Shark!' From that moment, it was all on.

I turned to the federal copper next to me and told him to call an ambulance straightaway. Then I jumped down on to the wharf, then down to the floating pontoon and showed Thommo where to pull the boat up.

When I saw Paul lying there, I thought he was dead. I've seen some dead bodies in my time and he looked like them: waxy and very pale. Then I saw that the back of his leg was missing and I thought, *Yes, he's dead, it's all over.*

But Thommo started slapping him around a bit and he coughed and spluttered and came to. They got him on to the pontoon and Lachy said they'd stuffed their T-shirts into the hole in his leg but that wasn't working, it was still bleeding. So I told Lachy to stick his hand in the back of the leg and pull the artery shut. Lachy slipped his bare hand in and held it as tight as he could. I found some rope on the pontoon and made up a tourniquet, and Lachy and I tied it around the leg, pulling it tight. I checked Paul's breathing and took his pulse. It was weak and thready, alternately racing and then losing speed – all typical of someone who's lost a lot of blood.

Paul was conscious at that point, but starting to suffer respiratory distress from the volume of blood he'd lost. We had a respirator there and put him on 100 per cent oxygen. A paramedic then arrived and took over.

The wharfies nearby built a ramp down to the pontoon. They were doing that quietly behind us, improvising with what materials they could find, while we were working on the leg. Then Paul was lifted up on a spine board into the ambulance that had arrived about 40 or 50 seconds after the first paramedic.

I followed the ambulance in the *HMAS Sydney*'s ship captain's car to the hospital. I just had to wait. Then I saw Paul briefly on his way to the theatre. He'd had a fair bit of morphine and made a joke as he went past. I think we were both feeling a lot better by that stage! At least I knew he was going to live.

I went back to *HMAS Waterhen* to have a coffee with the others. We'd all been very calm and clinical at the time, everyone doing exactly what their training had taught them, but the stress of the situation was by then starting to manifest. There was a fair shaking of hands around coffee cups.

### Able Seaman Clearance Diver Arthur McLachlin (Lachy)

I'd been in the water a while when Paul said he'd finish off the swim for me. I'd known him for less that a year – I was quite new – but that seemed typical of him. He's a very good bloke. And it was probably very lucky for me that he did that, although not for him . . .

I was driving the boat and we heard him shouting and saw thrashing in the water. I gunned the boat over to him and saw the shark's fin come up. We got Paul in the boat and we were pulling off gear to pack his leg. It was a massive, massive wound. At one point I thought he must be dead.

When we arrived at the pontoon, Patto came down and we could see where the blood was coming out. He told me to hold the artery tight to stop it flowing. It's something I hope I never have to do again. But at the time, I didn't think about it. I just did everything I could to give him the best chance – and I knew he'd do exactly the same for any of us.

Afterwards, someone said I'd had such a lucky escape, I should buy a lottery ticket. The experience has definitely made me a lot more cautious in the water.

# 18

## SO HAPPY TO STILL HAVE MY LEG

When I woke up in the Intensive Care Unit (ICU), I really wasn't too sure what was going on. I couldn't move. I couldn't speak. All I could do was breathe and look at the blur of motion around me. I remembered a trip to the UK when I'd snuck into a building to use the toilet, but once inside I realised I was in the middle of a Salvador Dali exhibition, and ended up staying an hour. The paintings were so vivid and incredibly surreal – animals and landscapes that twisted the mind and made you look harder at a world that couldn't possibly exist.

There was one quote from the exhibition I remembered: 'I don't take drugs; I am drugs.' That's how I felt in the ICU. The world had turned into something that I couldn't quite comprehend because my body was supported by drugs. But I wasn't worried or stressed. I hadn't fully grasped the situation and I wasn't in any pain, so I just closed my eyes in contented resignation and went back to sleep. I had no idea what was going on; everyone else filled me in later. Since I was either unconscious, asleep or out of it on drugs during that period, I'll leave it to them to describe what was happening. For me, only one memory remains clear: as I drifted in and out of consciousness during those first two days, I remember waking at one point and noticing I still had my leg. I was very happy about that.

### Dr Kevin Ho, plastic, reconstructive and cosmetic surgeon

With a shark attack these days, if the victim's still alive by the time they get into an operating theatre, there's a good chance they'll survive. If they're going to die, usually they die in the water from blood loss. Paul was very lucky. There are some huge blood vessels in the leg and if the shark had got the main trunk of one of those, Paul would have lost much more blood, he would have died there and then. But the shark missed one of those major blood vessels by just a couple of millimetres.

When I arrived at St Vincent's Hospital, Paul was under anaesthetic. The trauma surgeons had him on the table and had prepped him. My job was to decide which parts of his body could be saved, which had to go, and what else could be done to help.

Paul's right hand was a no-brainer. There was barely anything left from where the shark had taken his wrist; just bone sticking out through the end of skin and two crushed, useless fingers. If you're going to replant tissues, you need blood vessels going in and out and enough structure to provide a good functional outcome. With his hand, there was no structure that could be salvaged and no blood vessels. So it was an easy decision to amputate at the forearm and close the skin over, so a prosthetic could later be used.

His right leg was more complex. He'd basically lost all the back of the thigh and, most importantly, the sciatic nerve: the biggest peripheral nerve in the body, which begins in the lower back and runs down the leg, supplying movement to the leg and sensation for the sole of the foot. If you lose that nerve, the leg becomes effectively useless. It might look okay at first but inevitably without sensation there'll be ulceration and infection, which can make a person very sick and, ultimately, it'll need amputation.

Within 30 seconds of seeing Paul, I knew that so much of the sciatic nerve had gone – 22 centimetres – we'd have to amputate. I knew I could technically have reconstructed his leg's missing soft tissue, using skin and muscle from the other parts of his body, but it wouldn't be a good result. Even if he'd be able to move the leg afterwards, the movement would only be slight. It'd take three to six months in rehab to get even that and, at the end of it, he'd be carrying around pretty much a useless log for a leg, with no sensation, and he'd have to haul it around the place all the time. He would also have deconditioned his mind, and he would have lost a lot of his muscle bulk, which would affect his rehab potential. It would have really compromised the quality of his life.

In my job I deal with a lot of high-functioning athletes,

SAS types and clearance divers, and they tend to be very independent, decisive thinkers. I knew Paul would be exactly the same. When Paul woke from the first anaesthetic, he was in bed, looking at what seemed like a near-perfect leg – except for the defect at the back of his thigh and not being able to move his foot or feel anything. There was less to gain in me telling him outright he'd have to lose the leg. The best thing was for him to come to that realisation himself. For someone who'd always been in control of his life and body, this realisation was going to be the first and most major step in his decision to rehabilitate – or else debilitate. It was my job to give him all the information that would allow him to come to the correct conclusion.

## Kim Elliott, girlfriend

I was just getting ready for work that morning when I got a call from one of the boys in the boat to say that Paul had been attacked by a shark. I thought he was kidding. Probably a shark had just had a nibble and it wasn't anything major. But he sounded so serious, I knew something must be wrong. I asked if Paul was all right and he said no one knew. Then I realised with a shock that something really bad must've happened.

I jumped straight into the car and headed to the hospital. I called Dalla on the way to let him know, but it was hard as I didn't know much. I had no idea how badly Paul might be injured, or even if he was going to be okay. It was one of the worst journeys of my life.

At first the hospital staff wouldn't let me into intensive

care. They said the attack had been on the news already and I think they thought I might be a journalist. A nurse gave me a bit of a grilling and I started crying. I think then she believed me, and let me into his private room in the ICU. He wasn't in a good way. His temperature was all over the place and he'd lost a lot of blood. He looked terrible. His temperature kept going up so he had cold packs around him; his face was quite swollen and he had all these tubes down his throat. He looked awful but I was so relieved to see him alive. I'll never forget that feeling.

Then the surgeon, Dr Ho, came over and sat me down. He said Paul had lost his right hand and it looked like he was going to lose his leg as well. He said Paul's parents weren't there yet, so I shouldn't tell anyone. I said that no, of course I wouldn't.

**Dalla**

I still live in Canberra and was at home when I got a call from Kim. I looked on the net and saw the headline: 'Navy diver attacked in Sydney Harbour'. I jumped into the car and set off for Sydney. It was horrific not knowing whether or not your friend, someone you're so tight with, was going to live. Even to think about it puts me on the brink of tears. I just kept asking, 'Is he going to live? Is he going to live?' No one could answer me.

When I got to the hospital, I got straight in to see him. He was whacked off his head on drugs. But it seemed he was going to live, and he still had his leg.

**Matt**

When I got the phone call, I'd imagined Paul had fallen off his bike. When I found out what had happened, I was really shocked. I went straight to the hospital, and I'll remember that morning for my whole life. Paul was on all kinds of painkillers but he was still making jokes and flirting with the nurses. Kim wasn't amused, but he still had a sense of humour. He was so strong. His hand was gone, but his leg was still there.

I don't know how long I was out for, but the next time I woke I had a clearer vision of what was going on. There were friendly faces and worried smiles all around me. I tried to be reassuring but I still couldn't speak. I couldn't even close my mouth. I had tubes that looked like they were hanging from every orifice of my body, and there were hoses shoved in my mouth, halfway to my colon.

**Pat de Gelder**

I was in the staffroom of the hospital where I work in Canberra as the services manager when I got a call from someone in the navy. I'd seen the shark attack on TV and immediately said, 'You're not calling about that, are you?' He said he was, and that Paul was the one who'd been attacked and he was now in hospital. I asked if he was okay, but the man wouldn't say. So I knew it was serious. I booked a flight to Sydney and met Paul's dad at the airport to fly up together. At the airport I burst into tears, and didn't say a word all the way.

In hospital Paul was in a private room so I knew he must be bad. He had lots of tubes and drips, he was heavily sedated and you could see his hand was missing. That really affected me. I'd given birth to a perfect child and now he was missing something. His leg was all bandaged up and you could only see his feet. Sean came in to see him and when he went out into the waiting room, he put his head down and cried. That really upset me again.

## Sean de Gelder

I arrived after Mum and Dad, with my sister, Jacqui. Paul was in a pretty messed-up state. It was a shock. It was quite terrifying really. Just to see him lying there, helpless, with all those tubes in him. I didn't know what was going to happen.

## Dalla

It was distressing to see Paul like that but I didn't care. I was just stoked he was going to live. One moment, though, he had one life, then everything changed. But it seemed great he still had that leg.

# 19

## FUCKING SHARK

On my second day in hospital I woke up but I was still really drugged up. Apparently, I'd received over 300 units of blood – 17 times the amount of blood I'd had in my body originally, and around six times the quantity routinely given to someone in a bad car accident who's suffered massive blood loss. With the tubes still in me, some down my throat, I couldn't talk, but the nurses had drawn up a board with letters on it so I could communicate to everyone by pointing to the letters. It was very slow and frustrating. At one point I ended up throwing the board across the room because no one could keep up with my awesome spelling. Actually, I was so high, I couldn't spell for shit and kept getting words and letters mixed up. But I saw Kim and Mum and Dad were there, so I spelt out, 'Mum, meet Kim'. They all laughed. I guess they'd got to know each other already. Then I spelt out, 'Fucking shark'.

For pretty much all of that first week, I only remember waking up and then falling asleep again. I was in and out all the time. I hoped the tubes down my throat would only be there for a short time. Everything was very hazy.

## Kim

Paul spent a lot of the first two days unconscious in ICU. I sat by the side of his bed and kept telling myself that everything would be all right. He was still alive. But one of the first things that occurred to me was that he wouldn't be able to ride his motorbike, and I knew that would be hard for him as he loved it so much. It was such an emotional time; not knowing what was going to happen was so hard. The navy chaplain came and sat with me for a bit to make sure I wasn't falling to pieces. But I was very matter-of-fact about it. Later I bawled my eyes out a number of times, but never around Paul.

At one point, on that first day, the nurses told me to talk to Paul. They said he'd be able to hear me, even though he wasn't awake. So I leaned over and said, 'Hi!' But the nurses were still all looking at me, and one said, 'Tell him you love him.' I didn't know what to do; I'd never said that to him before. But I could tell the nurses were all thinking, *What's going on here? Boyfriend, girlfriend, and you've never told him you love him?* So eventually I leaned over again and said, 'I love you.' I thought, any minute now, he's going to wake up and punch me.

I had a lot of time to think about Paul, sitting by his bed. He was charismatic, and he made me laugh. I'd found him quite intriguing. We both liked training, but when we did it together, he'd nearly kill me in our beach sessions, getting me to run backwards in soft sand. We'd started hanging out more together but he was meant to be going away the next month and had been clear about not wanting to get into anything serious before he went. A couple of my friends kept saying, 'When he goes, you'll be a mess,' and urged me to go out on other dates. I went out on a handful with another guy but I think I was always comparing him to Paul. We just got on so well. But everything now had changed in an instant. It changed both our lives.

When other people started arriving at the hospital, I had to introduce myself to them. The navy had rung Paul's mum and said they'd been in contact with me, and his mum said, 'Who's Kim?' so when his parents arrived, that was an interesting introduction! More and more people kept arriving all the time. At one stage there were at least 40 people in the ICU waiting room, and a lot of them had travelled from beyond Sydney.

**Mark Hudson (Huddo), fellow navy clearance diver**

The first time I saw Paul in hospital he couldn't talk. I was emotional, very emotional. He's my mate, and to see him in that situation, and not knowing what was going to happen, it was a little bit overwhelming. I cried to see him like that.

He was trying to communicate with us, tapping out letters, but if he can't do anything, he gets so frustrated. There's normally nothing he can't do, so he was finding it very hard. He'd tap out letters, we didn't understand and he'd try to whisper but we couldn't hear. The effort exhausted him and he was so off his dial on drugs, he'd then fall asleep.

He'd been taught by an SAS guy when he was in the army to use rest as a weapon and he'd taken that and really run with it. When he'd go to sleep, he'd call it 'getting out his weapon'. In the army he needed it: he'd go on patrol with 30 kilograms on his back, walk for two days then go to sleep the moment he sat down. As clearance divers we'd be on a bus for two minutes, and he'd be asleep. We went one day to the firing range and there were all these loud cracks of gunfire and people roaring commands and all I could hear was someone snoring. I looked behind me and Paul was on the bench, fast asleep, despite all the noise. Then we woke him up, he shot a few aces, then went straight back to sleep again. In hospital I think that ability to sleep really helped him.

**Dalla**

I thought about how it was going to affect Paul's life, everything and everyone, from then on. It's a brainfuck. It does your head in. There's so much going through your head, you can't comprehend it.

But it was important to get over that, or push it aside for the time being, and get on with helping in any day-to-day, practical ways you could. With all those visitors, I would tell Paul that so-and-so wanted to visit and he'd indicate 'Yes' or 'No' on his board. He had quite a few girls he'd been seeing, and said they shouldn't come but some turned up anyway. Some I tried to shepherd away. One girl came three days in a

row and didn't get in. For me, it was all about trying to keep
both Paul and Kim strong. I didn't know how Kim would take
the situation. She's very open-hearted but she'd never had to
deal with anything like this. But she was great; she obviously
gave a shit. She was right next to Paul all the time.

## Kim

Everyone wanted to see Paul but when the hospital staff said
on the second day that only two people at a time could go in,
it got out of control, with people waiting hours and hours and
then getting in for five minutes, and then the doctors saying,
'No more!' So Dalla and I ended up in charge of crowd control.
I put everyone's numbers in my phone and people would text
me to ask what would be a good time to come, and ask how
many people were in the waiting room. After two days, Paul was
transferred to the navy ward at the hospital – the navy's own
hospital at Balmoral was undergoing work so it had a special
unit at St Vincent's – and they took the tubes out of his throat
so he could talk again. This time they said three people were
allowed in his room at any one time but, at one point, there
were 12 people there and every time a nurse came in, they'd
all scurry to hide in the bathroom.

Then a number of Paul's ex-girlfriends turned up too. It
was awkward with me in the room and I kept trying to leave
but Paul would ask me to stay. All these flowers kept arriving
too from different women. I told Paul about the flowers and
he was saying, 'I want you to be my girlfriend, I want you to be
my girlfriend,' and I was saying, 'Yes, I know. It's all right . . .'

There were still a lot of people coming to visit me but I couldn't cope with them all so I kept my closest friends or the boys from the dive team in the room with me as a buffer against them. They just hung out and talked shit and treated me normally. They cheered me up. Huddo would come in and he'd have a beer; I'd have a shot of morphine. I remember my chief coming straight up to me and kissing me on the head. I felt really weird, my chief kissing me. He had tears in his eyes, but I thought, *Shit! What are you doing?!* I said, 'Thanks, but let's not do that again, Chief . . .'

Another person I saw was Glenn Orgias, the surfer who got attacked by a shark the day after me. He'd been surfing the break off South Bondi in the evening. I saw him and apparently waved a piece of toast at him across the ICU. He ended up losing the same hand as I did.

### Sean de Gelder

There were so many people at the hospital waiting to see Paul. He had non-stop visits – all his friends wanting to see him. I stayed in Sydney for about a week but sometimes I'd sit in the hospital for the whole day and not see him, or there'd be two minutes at the end.

### Steve de Gelder

The first thing Paul said to me in hospital, using that alphabet board, was not to put off going overseas to work – I was about to take up a job with Abu Dhabi Customs in its risk-management division – just because this event had happened. He said he'd feel bad if he thought I'd turned down the opportunity of a lifetime because of his accident. He was so adamant, I did end up going. But that's indicative of his concern for others over and above his personal issues and welfare.

He's never been one for personal histrionics. Even as a toddler, when a dog tore his nose apart, he didn't let it overly bother him or interfere with his life. He just accepted what had happened and got on with being Paul.

## Kim

Paul was still so drugged up in that first week. There'd be a few conversations going on at once and it was too much for him to take in. Someone brought in a big box that Huddo's parents had sent and, when the top was opened, a big red helium-filled balloon on a string bounced out of the package, like a jack-in-the-box. It had a big smiley face on it and a hat, and it just sat there bobbing and smiling and never blinking – and Paul didn't like it at all. It freaked him out. Someone else brought in a teddy bear and Steve was being stupid, dancing the bear on his bed and Paul started saying, 'Get the bear off me! Get the bear off me!' We'd been joking around but he couldn't handle it.

On Valentine's Day, three days after the attack, Paul organised for one of the boys to sneak a beautiful bunch of flowers into his room for me before I arrived at the hospital that day. He also got a card, which took him around 15 minutes to write as it was the first time he'd used his left hand. He wrote the sweetest message: 'Kimmy, sorry my writing is spastic but I can't write with my left hand. I can't express how much you mean to me, I don't think I would have got through this without you. It would make me so happy if you would be my Valentine. I love you lots. Paul.' I still have that card and will keep it forever.

When he was able to talk again a couple of days after he was admitted, he kept saying he was so glad he had both his legs. He told the doctor he'd just learnt to surf, so he needed both legs. I remember looking at him and thinking, *He's got no idea how bad things are*. I didn't want to tell him because he was so happy to be in that place. And the doctors wanted to wait until he had his wits about him. If they'd told him when he was still so drugged, he mightn't have remembered later.

The doctors were coming in every day and touching the bottom of his left foot and saying, 'Can you feel that?' and he'd say, 'Yes.' Then they'd touch the bottom of his right foot and ask him if he could feel that, and he'd say, 'Yes.' Then they'd ask him where they were touching it, and he'd say, 'At the top' – while they'd been touching it at the bottom. So they knew.

The doctor finally said to Paul it was completely his decision, but if he chose to keep the leg, it would be useless and the wound at the back would take a long time to heal because it was so deep. He said they could do skin grafts over the leg but it would still be like a dead weight, with no feeling because the nerve had gone. It could catch on fire and he wouldn't know. Or they could take off the leg and patch him up and in a year's time he could be up and running with a prosthetic leg.

**Dr Ho**

Elite athletes and driven people like Paul see reason easily. They break down a problem into finite piecemeal bits and make decisions pretty quickly and accurately. It's part of their make-up and training. Paul needed to find out the facts and take control of his situation. I knew it would be very hard to hear a doctor saying he'd need amputation above the knee, but he had to know.

I talked to him about his leg and explained how useless it would be and what reconstruction would give him. I needed to give him all the facts so he could come to the right decision. It was a huge decision to make. He thought about it for a few days.

I still didn't know what was going on with my leg. I knew my hand was gone because I'd seen it missing while I was in the water but I was holding onto the fact that the surgeon I'd bribed with a case of beer on the way to emergency to save my leg really wanted that carton. I knew the leg hadn't gone and I thought, *It's still there; I'll be fine.*

But then the doctor came to my bed and explained that the shark had taken my whole hamstring, including 22 centimetres of my sciatic nerve, which was why I couldn't move my toes or feel my foot and parts of my leg. I started to get a bad feeling about what was to come and mentally prepared myself for the worst-case scenario.

The doctor continued, saying that I could keep my leg but due to the massive amount of damage it would essentially be useless, akin to lugging around a lump of wood from the hip – or I could have it amputated. I was crushed.

At that moment, my life took a massive pivotal swing and a million different scenarios started to flash through my mind. A life of hopping from place to place, wheelchairs, people staring, the pity, the sadness . . . The hardest thing was that the leg was there, and I just wished I could feel it but I couldn't. Dalla went off and did a lot of research and said one day, down the track, technology might allow me to make the leg work again. But I couldn't sit around just hoping that one day they'd be able to do something. In the meantime the leg would take months and months to heal, there'd still be a huge chunk out of it and I'd be dragging it around for years.

And then everything became clear: they could have the leg, and they could turn me into a Terminator or at the very least Steve Austin, the Six Million Dollar Man. The doc told me without my leg I could be mobile and running within a year. I'm not one to screw around. I said, 'Yeah, let's do it! Take it!'

**Dr Ho**

By saying we should take the leg off, Paul took the decision to get control back over his life. And for rehab, that's the hardest part done.

**Pat de Gelder**

We were all devastated, but Paul was so strong. He told the doctor to take his leg and make him bionic. He was making jokes even then. I don't know where he gets his strength from.

## Matt

I was really upset. I knew they wanted to take Paul's leg and I didn't think he'd be able to cope. He's such a physical person with the gym and riding his bike. I was really worried.

I was set to have my leg for just a week. It was wrapped in a type of vibrating bandage that helped with the circulation, and underneath you could see every detail of the shark's teeth in the marks it left. But day by day I watched my leg go darker in colour and become less lifelike.

In the days before the operation my amazing friends did their research and assaulted me with information and pictures to prove that life would go on as normal. I found out later that everyone had made a pact not to cry in front of me as it might make things harder for me. I appreciated that.

In my mind if there's a problem, then there's always a solution; it's just a matter of approaching it the right way. This, to me, was no different. There had to be an answer, some sort of fix so everything could go back to normal. Of course, I was on massive amounts of morphine and had a ketamine bulb permanently pumping horse tranquillisers into me, which puts you into a kind of dream-like state to kill some of the pain, so I wasn't exactly seeing things clearly. But no matter how hard I tried to go around, over, under or through my problems, I just couldn't come up with an answer. There seemed to be absolutely no way out and I began to feel like my life was over.

But then those survival instincts that we all have started to kick in. *Fuck it*, I thought. I could either curl up in a ball and harp on about my woes and how hard life is, alienate everyone I love and have a shit life – or I could improvise, adapt and overcome like I'd been taught. This was no time for fear. I'd had a great life and I'd be damned if I was going to roll over and die now. I knew the world would keep on turning with or without me so I'd best brace up and prepare to face it.

### Kim

I was with Paul the night before the op. We were lying there and he was looking at his leg and I said, 'Would you like me to take a photo of you now, with both legs?' He said okay. So he held up his leg and I took the photo. Ironically, the way he held it, the photo made it look as though he already only had one leg.

# 20

## WHAT'S NEXT? WHAT'S NEXT?

I was really focused on my leg at this point. From the moment I first noticed my hand was gone, when I was in the water, I'd accepted that. There was nothing I could do about it. It was hard, but I knew there was no point dwelling on it. I'd just focused on keeping my leg. And now, finally, that wasn't to be. I realised I really didn't have much of a choice. I had to go under the knife.

**Kim**

Paul had an awful, awful reaction to the drugs coming out of the amputation surgery. He really went into a black hole. When he went into theatre, a navy medic was holding his hand and Paul was holding it so tight, not letting her leave his side, that he nearly broke her fingers. The next day she came in with her hand all strapped up.

When Paul came round, he was in a bad way. His leg above the knee was really swollen and he was in agony. But while we could see he was really struggling, he still didn't complain about what had happened. I've never known him to say, 'Poor me!' It was always just, 'What's next? What's next?' If it had happened to me, I'd probably have been in a foetal position in the corner crying for months, thinking, *Oh my God, my life's changed so much*. But he never did.

I was tripping on the drug ketamine as I went into theatre and everything went white. I couldn't see or hear anything. Then my vision went black and I thought I must have died and gone to Hell. The medic said afterwards that she'd never heard anyone swear like me in her life.

I was in so much pain, I was off my brain. They'd changed the medication, I think, taking me off the hardcore morphine and putting me on a substitute, and my body wasn't ready for it. It was disastrous. They'd also moved me to another room, sharing with other people. They'd put me by the door and it was so noisy I couldn't sleep. One guy was dying and he was vomiting all the time, and I just had a curtain around my bed. I felt like I was surrounded by bad stuff. At one point I remember crying my eyes out for eight hours straight, the pain was so bad. A physio came through the curtain one time, saw the state I was in and backed right off. I think he thought it was all too hard.

## Pat de Gelder

Paul has always been someone who could take enormous amounts of pain so I was horrified when I saw him hurting so much. I hadn't seen him cry since he was a small boy. He asked me to go and buy him a gun so he could shoot himself. When the pain-control management team came in to assess him, I told them they had to give him something; this was crazy. They didn't seem to be doing anything so I told them if they didn't fix this, I'd go and get my car and run them over. I was told they didn't appreciate the threat. I left, crying my eyes out. Paul had 20 hours of that incredible pain until they got it under control.

## Dalla

We were all trying to keep Paul's spirits up. When the pain weakened a bit, Paul was eager to try to do everything he could to speed up his recovery, so straightaway we talked about what training he could do in bed to start moving again. I know what it's like mentally if you want to train and you can't. The physical stuff is important, but the mental stuff is important too.

## Dr Ho

With a situation like this, you can go one of two ways: give up, where you feel your life is over and you allow yourself to spiral down into depression, or overcome the odds, where you take control and make the best of things. From what I knew of Paul, I believed he'd fall into the latter category. I just needed to give him the best result so he'd believe it too.

We amputated his leg just above the knee and then took the spare tissue and skin and flipped it over what was left of the leg like a lid to reconstruct his thigh. The day after the op I came into the ward and found him doing chin-ups on the bar above his bed with his one good arm. I was shocked. He was in a lot of pain at the time, but he was doing the exercise presumably partly to take his mind off the pain. But I didn't think that was good. He could be shearing open the wound on his leg from the reconstruction. That was the first of many situations where I'd have to pull Paul back from doing too much.

**Kim**

Paul immediately asked Dr Ho, 'What's next? What happens now? Is there something I can do to make my recovery quicker? How can I strengthen myself so I can start to wear a prosthetic leg?' Dr Ho said that when he felt a bit better he could try to move his stump up and down a little to get some small degree of movement into it slowly. Paul said, 'What, like this?' and lifted his stump straight into the air, 90 degrees. Dr Ho's face just dropped in amazement. 'I can't believe you can do that already!' he said. Some people had been in physio for months after similar surgery and they could still only move a couple of inches. Then Dr Ho went off to get his video camera so he could film it.

**Dr Ho**

Most amputees have trouble initially moving that limb because there's a lack of strength there, they're inhibited by the pain and they need to retrain their mind to use that limb a certain way. But Paul had really, really strong buttock and hip muscles and, like top-conditioned athletes or people in the elite forces, he has an exceptional ability to control his body and use his mind to break through pain barriers in a way that most of us would find near impossible. He'd do things that are miracles all the time for the rest of us. The more I was getting to know him, the less I was surprised by him.

But you wonder what goes on in Paul's mind when he's by himself. On the outside Paul is the conqueror; he has an aura of invincibility. He wouldn't like anyone to know if he was struggling. But if anyone challenges him or says there's something he can't do, he'll try to prove them wrong for the rest of his life.

Every time I told him to rest, I doubled the time I'd tell him as I knew he'd immediately halve it. If I said the average person heals in ten days, he'd try to heal himself in five. And I always tried not to tell Paul he was doing better than expected as that was just a green light for him to push the boundaries even more. He's like that.

The navy at that point sent a counsellor to talk to me. After a few minutes I asked her to leave. I think she was quite shocked but she didn't know me and she didn't seem to know much about my situation. I had good friends to talk to, which I knew was going to help me a lot more. They knew me and I felt far more comfortable with them. I knew they'd tell me the truth whether I liked it or not. I wasn't running away from what had happened but I just didn't need a well-meaning stranger trying to counsel me. What happened had happened. I realised where I was and accepted it. I knew there was no way out. I couldn't grow myself a new hand or a new leg however hard I tried – and when I'd been zonked out on morphine, I really did try! But I just wanted Kimmy and the boys around me, and I needed to look forward to what I was going to do with the rest of my life.

I couldn't lie still in bed all that time either. I started hopping around the hospital. People seemed a bit surprised. Some of the nurses actually tried to confine me to bed. Fat chance.

### Kim

Paul had drains and tubes coming out of his leg for ages to collect the excess liquid from his body, trying to adapt to having the skin and muscle from the bottom half of his lost leg filling the hole in his thigh. The hospital eventually gave him a walking frame and crutches to get around but he didn't like them much. He preferred to hop. I remember the nurses having a heart attack. They told him he couldn't hop, but he wouldn't listen.

### Dalla

Paul had a lot of questions he wanted answered, so I made it my business to find out stuff for him. He wanted, for instance, to know if it'd ever be possible to ride a motorbike with one leg – answer: perhaps one day. He needed to know what modified bikes might be available – answer: a few, depending on a person's limitations. He needed to know if the navy would hold his job open for him – yes, they said they would. He was keen to find out how long he'd have to wait for a prosthetic leg before he could walk – and run and swim – again; it was being organised for him as quickly as possible. He just had to know, when he got out of hospital, what his future might look like. I arranged meetings and did research and did almost the power-of-attorney kind of stuff for him.

I just needed to get hold of all the information I could to know how I was going to get on in the future. I was also receiving dribs and drabs of information about that shark in the harbour all the time. The police had fished a body out of the water by the Woolloomooloo Finger Wharf the day before – a man who'd either committed suicide or fallen in – and that, no doubt, had attracted sharks. There'd been a cruise liner in that day as well and if they'd been dumping rubbish in the harbour, sharks could have followed that in. There was a ban on shark-fishing at the time as the annual quota had been reached. The sonar might have had some kind of effect on the sharks, you never know, and a fishing guide who was always there was saying fishermen had seen a lot of 7-metre sharks around there in the days before the attack.

I was amazed. Fishermen see us in there diving all the time – why the fuck didn't any of them think to mention it? The navy had assessed the shark risk as low at that time. But perhaps it was low risk for divers; I had been swimming on the surface and, statistically, sharks attack swimmers more than divers, and I had been dressed all in black with a couple of fins on, looking to all the world like a good feed. That shark probably would have been a lot less likely to attack me if I were diving. Not long after the attack, someone caught a bull shark of a similar size to mine, so it sounded as if he didn't end up having too good a day either.

### Huddo

I spent a lot of time in hospital with Paul. We all think about sharks when we work, but if you thought about them too much, you wouldn't be able to do the job. There've been shadows that have swum past me in the water in the middle of the night, but you try not to think about them. If you let them get to you, then you'd have to get out of the water, and you can't do that.

My first time back in the water was a week or two after the attack. My chief thought it would be funny to get a little shark from the fish market and throw it in. I'm glad he didn't – he'd still have the black eyes.

It was so great to be surrounded by the boys so much of the time, just talking shit, sitting around. It made me feel so much more normal. All that support was terrific for me. It really helped me get through everything. Their positive attitude helped me tremendously.

Two weeks after the shark attack, I'd mentally accepted the situation, but I still needed to know how I was going to manage, practically, without a right hand and right leg. I had no idea.

# 21

## CHOOSING LIFE

Everyone was saying I should lie in bed and rest, but I really wanted to be up, doing things. My whole life had been about running and jumping and swimming and moving and staying active, and I couldn't just give up now and lie there like a cripple. I might hop to the bathroom and fall over and then think, *Fuck! How do I get up now?* but I just needed to get moving. People kept telling me to slow down and that it wasn't normal to be so active after everything that'd happened, but I just ignored them.

I knew I had an excellent doctor in Dr Ho. From the moment I met him he just filled me with confidence. He had what I needed: a calm, clinical approach to my situation. Generally, if someone tries to take a roundabout approach with me I can tell instantly and it pisses me off. I feel their motivations are not pure and that they don't have enough respect for me, to be honest, which means that they, in turn, will be treated the same way. Dr Ho, however, gave it to me straight. He gave me the information I needed to know so that I could make plans and have confidence in what was to come. He also pulled me away from the brink of death, which takes you pretty far in my book. All of that aside, I had goals to kick, bridges to cross, rivers to swim and so on, and I felt I just didn't have time for three or four weeks of sitting on my arse, waiting to get better like he tried to advise.

Before each of my many surgeries the doc would tell me how much recovery time I'd need. I'd nod and smile and tell him, 'Sure thing, doc, no worries.' And in my head I'd just be thinking about being back at work and swimming as quickly as possible. He knew. I'm sure we had an unspoken understanding. He'd tell me how much recovery time I'd need and I'd do pretty much what I wanted unless it hurt so much I needed to rest. I know my limitations and I did take precautions, but you know what? I'm busy. I had things I needed to get on with and do.

Dalla was great. Now he was working as a personal trainer and a remedial massage therapist after going back to college, and he was also training in clinical hypnosis. He worked out what I could do to exercise while I was still in bed – if I pulled myself up like this, I could exercise these muscles; if I did weights like this, I'd be exercising those; sit-ups were possible, ab crunches, a modified type of push-up, one-arm chin-ups on the handle that's meant to be for helping you sit up in bed . . . Kim and my old mate Brock hauled in weights from my apartment in Bondi and Dalla brought me resistance bands that we tied all around the bed so I could do exercises with them. I charmed some of the nurses into giving me double portions of food to help build myself up again and asked for plenty of water. Kim lugged in a massive 5-kilogram bag of protein powder supplement and tins of rice and tuna to keep me going.

Physically, things were difficult. Apart from the pain of my injuries I was also wrestling with phantom sensations in the limbs that weren't there. I had a kind of pins-and-needles feeling in my missing hand and leg all the time, 24 hours a day. There were also intermittent phantom pains that were like huge bolts of electricity running all the way down my missing leg and into my missing foot that, each time they happened, made me stop and draw my breath. I might not have any for a couple of days, then I'd have six in half an hour. Every time they'd halt me in my tracks. Dr Ho told me such pains were common in amputees, especially those whose injuries resulted from trauma. Explained in layman's terms, they were due to errant signals being sent to the brain from the nerves in the injured limb. They can be difficult to eradicate but often can be successfully controlled by pain specialists.

I was beginning to realise how difficult it was to do the everyday stuff you don't normally think about. Getting up out of bed was hard; I'd have to sit up and roll and then wait for the pain to subside before I could put my left foot on the ground. Brushing my teeth felt like an almost impossible task. Writing now with my left hand when I'd been right-handed all my life left a mess like a spider on crack had been at the ink. And how the hell do you tie shoelaces or cut steak with one hand, or swim in a straight line with only one leg?

There were so many physical challenges ahead but I knew

I had to get going on my recovery as soon as possible and, if I was ready to go mentally, force my body to do stuff. It might not always be the best thing for my body, but that mental recovery was crucial. If you feel better, you're going to heal quicker. Even if you overdo things at first, and do a bit of damage to your body, you can heal later. The most important thing is how you feel about yourself. It was a struggle remaining optimistic and I knew I needed to tap into positive vibes as soon as possible. I wanted to be around strong, encouraging people who were going to urge me to keep going, rather than hold me back.

After that excruciating pain post-surgery went away, I could deal with the rest of the pain as I'd been through so much before. Being beaten up by bullies as a kid, those pack marches, throwing myself out of planes, getting gassed, running, training at the gym, that CDAT course . . . all those experiences helped me push through the pain barrier time after time.

I think you have to be a driven person, a Type A personality, to be in the defence forces, to train to go out and kill people. That now stood me in good stead. Instead of worrying about what I *couldn't* do, I focused on what I *could* do. The stuff you can't do any more? Forget it. Move on to the shit you can do and then, later, when you're more prepared, go back and learn to do the stuff you can't. Knowing that I'd once done those things, and remembering how it felt then, helped me.

Besides, I always knew it could have been so, so much worse. That made it easier somehow to accept my situation. I was comparatively lucky; I could still function to a high degree. There are people with much greater problems who have to rely on others to get by. I knew I could get back to being independent: I had beautiful friends around me and, two weeks after the attack, I had a meeting with the navy and was told I'd have a job with them as long as I wanted one. I think, however, they thought I'd be happy with a desk job. They didn't realise I wanted my old job back, doing all the things that clearance divers do.

The Department of Veterans Affairs also came forward with an offer for compensation; the subject of that DSTO waiver never came up again. At that stage I was still on a lot of drugs and I was never terribly clear about what I was signing when I agreed to their deal. But it seemed okay at the time – the navy would pay for all my medical care and prosthetic needs and also give me a modest cash amount. But, to be honest, I wasn't in any mood to bargain. I constantly wanted to move on, move on and move on.

All the while I was in hospital I ate to try to get my strength up, trained with the weights and bands, and learned how to use my laptop with just my left hand so I could do research on the internet and work out options for my day-to-day life. I also taught myself how to write with my left hand and tried to work out loads of little things, like how to put toothpaste on a brush and how to tie shoelaces, with only one hand. My flat in Bondi was a bigger problem. It was over a shop with two steep flights of stairs and no lift, and the doc said I wouldn't be able to cope with climbing them on crutches, especially if I had any groceries to carry. I had to concede that this time he was probably right. I realised I'd have to find another place, still preferably close to the beach but either on the ground floor or with a lift. I looked at a lot of possibilities online and Kim emailed a lot of real-estate agents explaining my situation and then inspected possible places for me. In the meantime Brock, who'd been working as a chef in a restaurant at Coffs Harbour, said he wanted a change of scenery and fancied living in Sydney for a while, and would be happy to share a two-bedroom place.

One day an agent came back to Kim and said he had an almost-perfect apartment – apart from its one flight of stairs. She went and took some photos of the stairs to show me. I thought I'd be able to manage with a bit of help, so I took on the lease. Then Dalla, Kim, Dad and a family friend Tony packed up my old place ready for the movers to transfer everything into the new one. It was quite a task. Dad said I seemed to have accumulated vast amounts of paraphernalia on my travels with the army and navy.

Throughout that time I was still getting lots of visitors. I loved that as it took my mind off what was happening. The visitors worked hard not to let me dwell on my situation too, which was great. Kim would come in every day, usually in the evenings after she'd finished work, bringing in her Lean Cuisine and waiting for my food to arrive so we could have dinner together. Then we'd watch TV and she'd curl up next to me in bed – much to the disapproval of some of the nurses. One in particular couldn't wait until the clock struck 10 p.m. so she could officially kick Kim out.

Another day someone from the navy dropped by to present me with a cheque for $5000 that the crew from *HMAS Watson* had raised to help me with my rehabilitation and recovery; $2500 were donations from a mufti day and $2500 from the ship's welfare fund. I was really touched. That kind of support meant so much. At the same time a young boy who'd read about me in the newspaper, the son of a former ship's diver, sent me $50 from his pocket money to help. I was very appreciative but used it to buy him clearance diving mementos.

There still seemed to be a lot of interest in me from the press and public, probably because I was the first clearance diver ever to have been attacked by a shark – lucky me! The navy issued a couple of statements on my behalf. That was good, as it gave me a chance to broadcast my determination to overcome my injuries to get back to my job.

'I'm looking forward to rebuilding my life and taking on the new challenges I have to face,' I told them. 'Ultimately, I would like to return to what I love – navy diving.' It was also a way of thanking everyone who'd helped me so much, particularly Thommo, Dartie and Lachy, as well as the doctors, nurses and staff at the hospital.

But people wanted to know more, and *60 Minutes* approached me. They were offering big money, but the navy said it wouldn't look right to accept it; people might think the organisation wasn't looking after me. That made no sense to my ears. The navy didn't want to be seen not to be looking after me, but it wouldn't let me get money that could potentially help me. I was a little bit pissed off about that! But then I thought it could be worthwhile doing a story without being paid anyway. Maybe I'd be able to do a bit of good for others who were struggling with their own problems, show them that there was more to life and that you didn't have to be weighed down by thinking always about the things you couldn't do.

Peter Overton was doing the story; his camera crew filmed me in hospital and were going to cover my discharge and the few weeks that followed. I'd already decided not to go into a rehabilitation place. A friend had gone into one after an accident and said when he arrived, he brought the average age down to about 80. I felt I knew how to train myself to get back on my feet – or foot – quickly, so I preferred to take charge of my own fate at home. I knew exactly how far I could push my body and if something hurt, then I'd keep doing it until it hurt a bit more, then do it a bit more again, and then I might stop.

In retrospect I put that nine weeks in a hospital bed to good use. I had a lot of time to think. I'd always had a bit of an Aussie 'she'll be right, it'll come good' type of attitude but I knew there was no easy way out of this. I was in a pretty bad situation and I needed to work out how I was going to deal with it. It's a very easy thing to just give in and be a victim but I can't imagine that it's very rewarding. So I made a decision to do the exact opposite and, since I didn't have anything else to do, I started straightaway.

My army training really helped. I'd learnt to switch off my emotions as a way of dealing with bad things, with misery, death and potentially killing or being killed. That meant I didn't fall to my knees when I confronted hurdles, I didn't get emotional or too introspective; I just gritted my teeth and got on with clambering over them. Without the old mantra I might have stopped at my first obstacle. But with that driving me on, and help from friends, family, and the rest of the divers, I kept on my path, focused on getting my life back, and overcoming whatever other difficulties might stand in my way. Breaking the difficulties down into small, manageable steps seemed like the best way to begin to make them more controllable.

Aside from that I tried to turn the things that could potentially harm me into strengths. Anger, for instance. I could have got angry about what had happened, the sheer unfairness of it, the *Why me? Why now?*, and let that eat me up inside. Instead, I turned my anger into a force that drove me onwards.

I didn't want to give up my dream life, so I chose not to. I was encountering a lot of non-believers along the way, mostly doctors, physios or other bystanders who thought I should be taking things slower or that I wouldn't be capable of doing certain things. They meant well, and I was grateful for their help, but they soon learnt that's not how I operate.

So, on 15 April 2009, with a *60 Minutes* crew in tow, I refused to sit in a wheelchair, picked up some crutches instead, and finally left hospital, ready to start the rest of my life.

# 22

## ARE THEY NEW NIKES?

My homecoming felt very strange. I had the *60 Minutes* crew filming me walking in the door – although I'd never actually seen the flat before, so it didn't look much like home to me. I saw all my stuff there, which was great, but I felt a bit distant from it all. I was still on a lot of drugs anyway, so I wasn't really in top form. I remember seeing a pair of my shoes under the bed and going over to pick them up, then realising I wouldn't need both of them any more. I made a joke about it, but it felt very weird.

When the crew finally left, it was just me, Kim and Brock on our own. Brock served us up a big feed. After we'd finished eating I suddenly went into a downward spiral. Out of hospital, no longer with all those nurses, doctors and that big crowd of mates looking after me all the time, I guess it really hit me. I realised all the things I could no longer do for myself, all the things I took for granted. Without the hype and excitement of the TV crew there, cold hard reality had started to sink in. I went into my bedroom, sat down on the bed, put my head down and just bawled my eyes out. It's the only time, apart from straight after the operation when I was in so much pain, that I really cried.

I was just so overwhelmed. It hit me that this was now my life – missing a leg, missing a hand. I was literally half the man I'd been and I wished that I'd died. At least then I wouldn't have had to go through this torture. I couldn't take it; it was too huge a concept that I'd live the rest of my life like this. How would I drive or dive or do any of the crazy stuff I did before that I felt had made life worth living? There just didn't seem to be anything left for me; my life as I knew it seemed finished. It was a defeatist attitude and I hated myself for it. Previously, anything was possible and now everything seemed impossible. *What am I going to do now?* I asked myself, feeling pathetic.

But eventually I ran out of tears and, you know what? Nothing had changed. I realised that I could lie there, crying and sooking until the end of my days, but I'd still be *sans* limbs when it was all over. I'd still be hurting, I'd still be struggling and, since suicide was out of the question, I'd still be alive. So I asked myself again, *What the fuck am I going to do now?* I knew struggle and I knew pain – they'd been close personal friends at many times throughout my life – but now I no longer had any fear of death. In some ways that liberated me. I was free of the constraints that are imposed on us by holding tightly to our mortal coil. And that's how I decided to take it all on myself.

I would do my own rehab, I vowed, take myself off the

medication, get myself fit and strong mentally and physically. To hell with dwelling on the negative aspects. Negativity is a vacuum in which nothing else can exist. It has no usefulness, and I decided to ban it from my life. I had no fear of failure because, if I wanted something enough, I'd bite into it and hold on like a rottweiler at a dog fight until it was accomplished. I'd do all that I could possibly could not to fail. Life was tough so all I had to do, I told myself, was to be tougher. Of course, that was easy to say, but harder to do.

When I emerged from that little breakdown, Kim looked worried, but I reassured her: 'I'll get used to it, I'm fine, I'm fine.' Of course, I wasn't really fine. I felt like my old life had vanished and what was left had been turned upside down and inside out. But after feeling sorry for myself for a bit, I was determined to just get on with it and make the best of it all.

That first week, though, was tough. The hardest thing was getting out of bed every morning. In my mind I'd be bouncing out of bed, throwing on clothes, racing out for a swim in the sea and a run along the beach, and then hoeing into breakfast. In reality it would take me a long, long time to ease myself up, prise myself out of bed, get dressed painfully slowly and then hop over to the kitchen to work out what I could manage to eat.

An occupational therapist came round and organised things like a chair in the shower for me, and brought me gadgets, including a chopping board with suction pads so it'd stay on the work bench and a little rocker knife that made it easier to cut up meat. She was great. I think some people still find it hard watching me struggle with things like cutting food but there's not much

I can do about that. I'm determined to do everything myself and only if I really can't do something, will I ask for help. I don't like anyone making a fuss. I'd always rather find another way of doing something than give up. I learned to hold my toothbrush in the inside of my right elbow while I put toothpaste on. At dinner I'd apologise for my caveman technique as I'd stab a piece of meat with my fork, hold it up in front of me and bite chunks out of it rather than ever having someone cut up food for me as though I were an invalid or a child. It's hard to hop around with a bowl of breakfast cereal and juice so I'd often have breakfast standing in the kitchen instead. And with grocery shopping, it was easier to do it online.

I started off my rehab at what I thought was an easy pace. I trained every day as hard as I could and, in between my appointments with doctors and therapists, found ways of taking back my life. I had small goals that I constantly updated: do this exercise, walk that far, climb those steps, get up earlier, eat more, focus. I focused on what I needed, what I wanted and how to do it. Did I need to be functional? No, I needed to be better than functional. If I was going to be regarded as fit to perform my duties at work and live in the manner that I enjoyed, then I needed to be better than I was and, quite frankly, better than most people around me. I needed to work twice as hard to do things that others could do simply so I needed to practise three times harder to make it look effortless. 'Train hard, fight easy' echoed in my head.

Some days I failed. Some mornings I just couldn't bear to drag my arse out of bed and hop around the house, or, later, to put on my prosthetic leg and face the world. A world I knew would stare and ogle and whisper to their friends, 'Check that guy out!' I just couldn't do it. So I'd lie there and try to get back to sleep with the phantom pains gnawing away at me and my back aching. I'd feel guilty and depressed and sorry for myself all at once. Then I'd hear a whisper, just quiet at first: 'That weight's not going to lift itself.' And then a little bit louder, 'Dry your eyes, princess.' Then louder still, 'I'm not here to fuck spiders.' And then even louder, 'Build a bridge and get over it!' And, finally, almost screaming, ringing in my ears until I almost yelled it out loud to myself, 'Harden the fuck up!' Being weak was for everyone else, anyone else. I was a fucking soldier and I'd better bloody well act like it. And off I'd go.

But in truth I was still in a pretty bad way. I was still smashing a lot of drugs: Temazepam for sleep; OxyContin and Endone, which are morphine derivatives and often referred to as 'hippie heroin'; Epilim, an anti-epilepsy drug to manage the nerve pain I had but which, in fact, did nothing; and antibiotics. I felt like I was in a fantasy land half the time and I hated that, so I started cutting the painkiller dosage back. I felt like I had an enemy to fight but I couldn't fight it if I couldn't focus. I needed to be completely aware of my situation in order to know where to start my recovery and regain my life. But night-time was the worst, and that's when I needed the painkillers just to get to sleep. Sometimes I'd lie in bed for hours, rocking from side to side, close to tears with the frustration of it all. There were the simplest of things like sleeping or walking that I felt I couldn't accomplish. So how the hell was I ever going to drive or do anything that required complicated motor movements? Eventually the drugs would kick in and I'd be granted dreamless, painless bliss.

Sometimes during the days that followed, all I longed for was that sleeping time. No more pain, no more worry, no more anger. I just wanted to sleep and escape it all. Even in the first few minutes of waking up, I'd have a little bit of time to myself before the phantom pains would creep back and settle in to the hand and foot that weren't even there for me to rub. During the day I'd refrain from taking the drugs for as long as I could, for as long as possible, until it hurt so much that I had no other choice but to dose up.

I still managed to come off all the medication faster than the doctors told me to. By the time they suggested starting to ease back on them, I was almost drug-free. I just didn't want the meds to rule my life or to become addicted to them in any way. I'd rather deal with the pain. I think eventually the doctors understood that I was a really hard-headed bastard, and you could tell me to do something till the cows come home, but if I wanted to do something my way, then I was going to do it.

I was trying hard to get my life back together. Brock was an amazing help – he cooked for me, cleaned and helped me with things until I learned how to do them myself. My other friends were all offering assistance too, but I found it very hard to ask for help – always have. But with Brock there, it made it easier. Then, after breakfast each day, he'd drive us both to the gym at the Victoria Barracks army base in Paddington so I could continue working out and build my strength and fitness back up. It would usually be very quiet there, which I liked as I was pretty self-conscious. We'd train for about two hours every day and I had to improvise a lot of exercises as one leg and hand can really throw out your bench presses and dead lifts.

My arm was healing up well but it was still very sensitive and it hurt to put weight on it. That meant I couldn't do push-ups, for instance. So I'd drive my stump into a punching bag, or the soft pad of the armrest on the pec-deck gym machine used for building up the chest, over and over again, doing it harder and harder as the weeks went on to toughen it up. I knew it was just going to take patience and determination to get where I wanted to be, and I knew eventually I'd get there. I'd do it every day until it hurt too much to continue, and then move on to something else. Next, I'd maybe do a one-handed push-up with my right elbow resting on the padding of a low bench or dips just using my shoulders in the Roman chair for leg raises.

In those early days there wasn't a lot more I could do after that. Living at Bondi Beach, I really didn't want to go out too much because I got sick of dealing with the stares. I got down to the beach a few times but mostly it was just easier to stay home and watch a movie or do some Wii boxing. It was a slow process and often I'd get annoyed at how long it was taking.

### Kim

It was so hard watching Paul go through his rehab. That first night when he had his little breakdown, I could see he wasn't coping but I didn't know what to do or how I could help to make it better. I found it distressing but I didn't want him to know. It wouldn't help him.

In the end I decided to take him away for the weekend, to get away from it all. We couldn't go far, so I booked a weekend in Manly. I think he thought it was a bit odd, but I felt I just needed to get him away for a couple of days.

With Paul the hardest thing was always *not* to help him. I'd struggle with that – and still do, to this day. I'd go to help, then pull myself back. He never wants help. He's so stubborn and insists on doing everything himself, whether that be putting on his belt, trying his shoelaces, cooking a meal. He's so patient, teaching himself to do things all over again, and refusing to 'need' someone to help, right from the beginning.

The first time we went over to my parents' place for dinner, Mum kept trying to help by pulling his chair out, or moving things closer to him. But he hates fussing. Then she'd look at me as if to say, 'Why aren't you cutting up his food for him?' If he has a chicken breast in front of him, stabs his fork into it, holds it up and then just bites bits off. He always seems to find a way. If he needs help, he'll always tell me, he'll ask for it. But that's quite rare. He prefers to struggle and get things done himself.

He does have down times, and I know it gets to him, but he doesn't talk about that very much. He knows it's really shit that he can't go out and do all the things he used to, but it's only when he's let his guard down, perhaps when he's had a few drinks, that he'll ever talk about it. He'll say he's only half a man, why would I want to be with him? But I always say the answer's simple: he's the same person I fell in love with; he's just missing a few bits now. I give him a little pep talk. But when he sobers up, he's back to normal and so determined to be upbeat, it's really inspiring.

As I started to get fitted for my prosthetics, I spent more and more time out in Sydney's western suburbs having sockets – the stump attachment system – fitted and shaped and practising using them. Then there'd be appointments with my occupational therapist, physiotherapist, and then hydrotherapy, check-ins at the hospital to update the navy doctors and pick up more drugs. I seemed to be in a constant state of appointment. On the plus side I was fully up to date on all the Hollywood gossip from spending so much time in waiting rooms. The girls would laugh at me because I'd get into a discussion about who was doing who and all the scandals of the week.

I'd been really impatient to get the prosthetic leg so I could start walking around again. The quicker I could get to grips with that, the quicker I could get a running leg and then a waterproof leg for swimming and surfing. Once the doctors realised how determined I was, they let me have a leg just a couple of weeks after I was discharged, before all the swelling had really gone down. When I practised walking in physio, they were amazed at how well I was doing and kept videoing my progress. In truth the pain from the pressure on the leg wound was terrible. Every night I was in agony and couldn't get to sleep without drugs. But I knew it would be worth it if I persevered. I just didn't want to be stuck sitting around. The doctors told me that my leg might never go back down to its normal size but it's not in my nature to just sit back to wait and see.

My walking leg, called a 'C Leg', was made in Germany. With an internal structure made of lightweight carbon graphite, titanium and aluminium, it's the most technologically advanced prosthetic leg available but it doesn't do everything. For starters, I can't run with it, neither can I walk up a step with it. I have to step up with my good leg and then bring the C Leg up to join it before repeating the sequence. It makes it quite hard to walk up a steep incline and extremely difficult to walk on sand. It's not water-resistant and if I lean on it at any angle it will collapse and I'll end up on my arse or head. But regardless of its shortfalls, it allows me to walk. It has a microprocessor in it – a computer chip, and a lithium battery below the knee joint which needs to be plugged into the wall or the lighter in the car for charging. The chip measures my weight distribution, speed and gait to make constant, automatic adjustments to the leg and now, after extensive practice, I can walk down any amount of steps without a handrail.

The structure then has a polyurethane cover to make it look a bit more like a real leg. Most people choose to have a flesh-coloured one but I chose black instead. If I was going to have a fake hand and leg I thought it better that they look like awesome fakes than like I'm trying to hide them. I usually wear shorts but if I'm wearing long pants you wouldn't even think I have only the one leg. Until I try and dance that is – and then it's all bad.

For my arm, the doctors agreed to give me a weightlifting hand first so I could exercise while I waited for both a standard hand and a waterproof version. That came a bit later than my leg, but it made it much easier to train. It allowed me to lock on a weight or hook over a bar. It had an interchangeable socket that could either go below or above my elbow, so I could push and pull, making it possible to do chin-ups, rows, military presses – lifting dumbells above my head to target the deltoids and triceps – bench presses, even a bit of basic boxing. It was a huge leap for me to be training effectively again and it spurred me on.

My regular prosthetic hand finally came in June. I have what is called an 'I Limb'. It's a myoelectric prosthetic and uses sensors inside the forearm socket to detect electrical muscle signals and move the fingers. It's the most advanced hand available but, like the C Leg, it has a long way to go before it even comes close to rivalling a real hand. Black again, and with robotic fingers, it's basically a very expensive and cool-looking holding device. It has no dexterity or planes of movement and without an expensive latex glove, generally most objects will slip through its fingers. It's slow, noisy, has no individual finger movements, and the thumb angle has to be conducted manually. It's also extremely delicate. So far I've broken it around eight times. It has to go to Scotland for repairs, which can take up to five weeks each time. Since I got it, I've actually spent more time without it than with it.

The sockets to which these hands are attached have their problems too. The only way to effectively hold the hand and sensors in place so they're functional is to have a socket that anchors above the elbow. This severely limits movement as you can't straighten your arm, making you look like C-3PO from *Star Wars*, Luke Skywalker's golden protocol droid, walking around with a perpetually bent arm. At the other end of the scale it is more useful than an arm with no hand, which is what I'd otherwise be stuck with.

A few months later I was fitted with a waterproof leg so that I could dive, swim and surf (badly). It can be used for other activities like snowboarding too, as the knee, unlike the C Leg's, doesn't collapse when leaned on. The knee joint, called an XT9, looks like the compression spring from a mountain bike. That, combined with an ankle that can unlock so that the toes of the foot can point in a particular direction, means I am back to semi-effectiveness in the water. But the fact that the knee doesn't collapse also means that it doesn't really bend, which makes popping up on a surfboard with a straight leg quite difficult, and locking and unlocking the ankle can be very ungraceful – especially when it locks up and doesn't want to move. Also, when I'm surfing, and look down to see where the leg is and that movement means I'm off the board again. Still, practice makes perfect, and I have a lifetime for that.

As well, I was given a running leg: a long, curved carbon-fibre leg that I knew worked because I'd seen people using it, but which looked to me like a mediaeval torture device. I tried it out once just before I had my latest surgery in November 2010. I looked more like a kangaroo having a seizure than anything else and promptly landed on my head. The surgery delayed me being able to try it out again, but I was looking forward to starting.

Although I often get the shits with my legs and hands when they break or rub the skin off my body or make me look like an invalid, I'm also thankful they exist. In the past I might have had to have a hook which, although very cool for dress-ups, could prove quite catastrophic. If you make a mistake saluting or scratching your nose on a bumpy car ride, you'd know all about it. But I've become pretty effective without my hand. Necessity, after all, is the mother of invention. That said, cooking without burning myself took a while to learn, I've broken more dishes than I own, and using a dustpan and broom has still got it over me. It's the simple things you don't expect that are the challenges. The amount of trouble I have trying to thread a needle and sew a button on my shorts is incredible, and infinitely frustrating. But like everything else, it gets done. It might not look pretty, but it gets done.

Kim spent a lot of time with me after I was discharged. It was kind of weird, our relationship. We hadn't been going out long before the attack happened, and I felt sure she'd finish things with me. This wasn't exactly what she would have had in mind when we started seeing each other. But she said later that it had never crossed her mind to break it off, not even once. A couple of people had asked her if she was planning to stay with me and she was shocked and offended and got quite shitty with them, apparently. She said I was the same person I'd always been, and that hadn't changed. She'd love me just the same if I'd lost both legs.

I was at home learning to walk with the first version of the prosthetic leg, when she came over and said she was taking me away for the weekend. I'd been a bit up and down and I think she wanted to get me out of myself. She knew I'd get restless just sitting in the car for hours, so we ended up going to Manly for the weekend. It was funny going from one Sydney beach to another for a couple of days, but it was great. We stayed in a nice hotel and had dinner there in the evening, and a room-service breakfast the next day. Depending on what there is on the menu, sometimes it's a lot more comfortable for me to eat at a place where other people don't stare.

My moods did continue to go up and down, though. Sometimes I'd feel fine, and sometimes I'd be a bit low. There were always times when I'd lie in bed in the morning and think, *I don't know if I can do this today*.

Dalla was always good to talk to at times like that. He'd say, 'If you feel like shit, allow yourself to experience the emotion, but don't feel shit all day. Don't let it ruin your life.' He told me to give myself room to feel low, but to never let it prevent me from doing stuff. That made sense to me. I've never been the kind of person to lock myself in a room and mope. I've always been, 'I'm here! Let's go!' I think that attitude had helped me get through so many things in my past, and seemed to make a huge difference to my recovery.

But the pain was exhausting. It was always there, like having a TV playing white noise in the background, slowly driving you insane, and I knew it'd be there the next day as well. Sometimes it made me close my eyes and hold back a cry, but then I just tried harder to tune it out. I didn't talk about it either because I knew I wasn't the only one with problems and I didn't want to be a whinger, so I kept it inside. I'd been trained to suffer in silence, to grit my teeth, ignore pain and eventually it'd subside. The problem was, it was never far away and I didn't know if it would ever stop.

In my old life I'd been invincible; there was nothing I couldn't do and if there was a problem I would find a way to make it better. I'd jumped out of planes as an army paratrooper with a machine-gun, bombs and a pack attached. I'd walked for days and nights patrolling jungles and bushland at home and overseas, hardly talking for days at a time. I'd fast-roped 30 metres out of helicopters with no more equipment than a pair of gloves and a plastic helmet. I'd swum kilometres at a time underwater in the pitch-black waters of night. I'd done some amazing things – and if I now didn't have the pictures to remind me, I might not have believed it myself. But those things now felt like fuck-all compared to what I was going through, and I wasn't sure if I'd ever come out the other end.

Every day, though, I felt more and more like I had a personal choice: to feel sorry for myself and end up becoming bitter and depressed and making the people around me miserable; or I could choose to have a good life, not let it get me down and never take my blessings for granted. When you think of it like that, really, it's not that hard a decision. Every day I needed to make sure I lived my life to the fullest. I'd think about the good things in my life and hold them close to my heart.

And there were so many high points. *60 Minutes* asked me if I'd like to swim with sharks for their show. I happily agreed. I was eager to get back in the water again, even the thought of being so close to sharks didn't bother me that much. We went to Manly's Oceanworld Aquarium. Getting kitted up, I felt a moment's hesitation . . . and then I got on with it. Swimming around felt great. It was wonderful to be back in the water. It was only when a 3-metre shark swam over me as I stood on the bottom of the pool that I felt a shiver. I found myself looking away from the front ends of the sharks. I'd look at their faces and have a picture in my head of one of them turning round with those big teeth hanging out of its head and tearing my face off. But I knew full well that wouldn't really happen since they were grey nurse sharks, which are fairly placid. But I was still much happier looking at the giant stingrays and the turtles.

Then the show said they'd teach me to drive again – in a Porsche on a racetrack. I loved that! It was an automatic so I didn't need to change gears but it was strange steering with just one hand at speed. While I used my left leg for the brake as normal, I had to push down with my hip to make my prosthetic leg work the accelerator. It was difficult at first, but it didn't take me long to get the hang of it. That was a real thrill. The show was broadcast on 8 May 2009, just under three months after the attack, and described me as a 'man in a million'. It was followed by a live online interview and people said such nice things to me; it felt really good and lifted my spirits no end. I thanked them all and said that by doing the story, I hoped I might help someone overcome their demons, or get past some hurdle in their life.

As I slowly encountered my own hurdles and climbed over them torturously, one by one, life steadily improved. I got better at walking on my new leg and, having never liked being cooped up inside, would go out more often, walking along the promenade at Bondi Beach. I noticed a lot of people staring at my prostheses, and a few obviously recognised me from *60 Minutes* and came up to say hello. Sometimes they were so friendly, it was nice, but it was hard to be reminded constantly of what made me different.

It wasn't long before I went back into the sea. I went down to North Bondi with Brock and another friend, Robbo, and our surfboards. My waterproof leg still hadn't arrived at that stage, so I had to hop along the soft sand with an 8-foot surfboard under my arm, and then hop through the water as well. It was really hard, but I was determined to do it. I had a latex socket over my leg and an old wetsuit on, and I paddled around having a great old time.

I didn't know it but I had been spotted by a paparazzo, who'd taken photos of me. They came out in the newspapers a day or two later, and the navy called me with a Please Explain, since I wasn't allowed to do any press without their permission. I told them I'd had no idea I was snapped.

It was difficult getting used to having one of my paddles missing and I had a picture in my head of me swimming round and round in circles. It took a bit of time to work out how to manoeuvre my body with just one arm. A wave would hit me and my board would go flying off behind because I could only hold on with one hand. Since I couldn't stand up on the board either, I just lay on it. But it was an amazing feeling to be completely immersed in the ocean again, and that overrode all the difficulties. I guess you can only really appreciate that if you've been brought up around water and are completely comfortable in it. If I got dumped by a wave and had to spend 30 seconds underwater trying to recover, it never worried me; I was quite relaxed, knowing I could hold my breath and bring myself up to the surface later. I felt fantastic being out there.

About that time someone from the navy called me into the office and said they had something to show me. They had a snippet of film of the shark attack from the sonar-detection test. I held my breath as it began, but it was a bit of a disappointment. The footage was black and white, and blurry and grainy, so you really couldn't see much. All I saw was a tiny dot that was me and a bigger dot that was the shark, a whole lot of splashing, and my fin going up and its fin going up, and not much more at all. It was odd that they were filming everything that day, but it was such poor quality. I was only allowed to see that part of the film and, to this day, have no idea whether that sonar device actually detected the shark in the water with me before it attacked. But to be honest I'm not bothered either way. What happened, happened. I'm only interested in looking to the future.

As I became more confident, my social life got back on track and I was happy to head out with my mates drinking again, going to parties, going for dinner with Kim and hanging out at the beach. There were plenty of other things happening too. One surprise was being asked to take part in a documentary, called *Day of the Shark* for the American Discovery Channel, about six survivors of shark attacks around the world. I was the first up, and they played some really creepy footage reconstructing the mauling I'd received. Again for the cameras, I was invited to make a 'celebrity' cameo in a TV commercial for VB that aired here during the Ashes in England in July 2009, alongside the likes of Michael Clarke, Wally Lewis, Scott Cam, Molly Meldrum and Michael Klim. And I suddenly started receiving requests to make speeches at various functions.

At first I turned those down. I just didn't feel like I was a public speaker. But then I was asked if I'd speak to a group of kids suffering from cancer for the charity CanTeen. Of course, I couldn't refuse them. The day I rocked up to do the talk, I was pretty nervous, as I'd never done anything like it before. But I took a deep breath and just told them my story. I showed them some of the gory photos of my injuries and they seemed to love that, and talked about the dangerous stuff I did in my job. I even took my prosthetic arm off halfway through, and passed it round for them to see and touch. When I'd finished talking, there was a moment of silence. It felt awkward and I wondered what to do next.

'Would anyone like to ask me a question?' I said. There was a lot of murmuring that seemed to go on forever until one young boy put up his hand. I wondered what the hell he'd ask me, mentally flicking back through everything again and promising myself that I'd answer as openly and honestly as I possibly could. These were innocent kids with a deadly illness. You couldn't bullshit them, and neither should you ever try. They knew, more than almost anyone else, what it was like to feel vulnerable, to stare death in the face, to fight to live. Standing there with them felt like yet another turning point in my life. To see kids so much worse off than me, kids who'd spent up to 12 months at a time in hospital with no hope of going home anytime soon, kids who'd lost both hands and both legs to meningococcal or bone cancer – compared to them, I was just so lucky. They were just teenagers but they were getting on with life.

I could see the boy taking a deep breath. I took one too. And then his question rang out through the room.

'Are those the new Nikes you've got on?'

The second question came from a kid who was holding my arm.

'How much is your watch worth?' he asked.

And the third question: 'Have you ever killed anyone?'

After all the questions I'd thought I might be asked, and all the answers I'd mentally prepared, once again I'd been completely blindsided. But at least this time, I could afford to laugh.

# 23

## DREAMING BIG

By August 2009, six months after the shark attack, I felt I was ready to go back to work. I had my new leg, my new arm and I'd regained most of my strength, health and fitness. My determination and drive to do my job to the very best of my ability remained undimmed. My mates and the other divers were all very encouraging; they'd known just how much it had taken me to get to this point. But the navy had its doubts.

As a clearance diver, you're among the cream of the defence forces. You can go anywhere and do anything. I knew that given a bit of time and a refinement of my prosthetics, I'd be back in the top 20 per cent of divers once again, despite having one black carbon-fibre hand and one black carbon-fibre leg, each with microprocessor-controlled components. But I also knew that the navy chiefs might have a few problems matching me with their ideal. They were keen to put me behind a desk; I was even more keen to avoid it. As you go up the ranks, you usually take much more of a supervisory role so your body's not under as much stress. But then you're not doing the cool stuff. I'd happily do the job of an able seaman or a leading seaman – what's known as a 'Kellick' – for the rest of my life.

I knew it was a big ask to become fully operationally deployable again, but I figured, why *not* dream big? I set out trying to prove myself all over again to my employer. From day one it was obvious they were going to put restrictions on the things I'd be allowed to do, but I set out to punch holes in those restrictions, one by one, day by day, week by week, month by month. My philosophy was always. Don't tell me I *can't* do something; ask me if I *can* do something and then I'll show you I can. Of course, it made me a pain in the arse to deal with at times, but I guess one of the reasons they hired me in the first place was because I was so pig-headedly determined. And after 33 years of being that way, I just wasn't prepared to change now.

After a lot of negotiation, the bosses agreed I could go back to work at the dive school, where the clearance divers are trained, at *HMAS Penguin* on Middle Head in Sydney's Balmoral. There I had to undergo a series of tests to be allowed to work in various capacities. One of the first was to check that I'd be okay on a dive boat. I was shocked they'd even think it might be a problem but, dutifully, I went along with it. Accompanied by a whole team of people, including a physiotherapist, two doctors, an occupational therapist and the boss of the dive school, I stepped onto the boat and stood on the deck as it was moving with no problem at all.

Standing there, as stable as anything, I couldn't help smiling when the physio stumbled and nearly fell flat on her back. Needless to say, I've progressed through all the tests I've been set so far and now even have my ticket to drive the boat. Yes, they started off saying I couldn't go on the boat, and I ended up driving it.

It was great to be back at work, and good to be back in the company of the other divers. By the start of 2011, the whole dive branch was on my side, and wanted me to get through all the tests so I could get my old job back. There were still plenty to go – being cleared for diving operations again, using weapons, munitions-clearing . . . But I know I'll get through them all. I have no doubt about that. Since returning to work I've even completed a helmet-maintainers course and can now completely disassemble, service and reassemble the diving helmets that the dive branch uses, even though they break down into hundreds of tiny pieces.

Around October 2010 I had a 'discussion' with the navy medic about why I should be allowed to be deployed overseas. I'd done lots of trips before and there was nothing I'd done on those that I'm not capable of now. The doctor, however, argued there was a risk of me falling over and hitting my head. I argued that there was a risk *anyone* could fall over and hit their head. We all operate on calculated risks. At one point he said, 'So you're not really going to try to get deployed, are you?' I looked him straight in the eye and said, 'Yes.' He looked and me and said, 'Oh shit!'

I know there might be a level that they are not going to allow me to reach, whether that's being deployable on exercises or deployable on operations. But all I can do is keep pushing down the barriers that are put up, usually by groups of faceless, nameless people who've never even met me, have no idea what I am capable of, like to bury me in endless paperwork and who seem to be the ones making the most critical decisions about my life.

It frustrated me. There was nothing I was doing at the dive school by mid-2010 that I hadn't done on exercise in Malaysia or Singapore. Occasionally, I might have had to find other ways to do something, but this just made me an even stronger member of a team. I'd have loved it if they'd just let me do everything and if there was something I couldn't do, then I'd go to them and we'd work it out, but that's not the way the forces operate.

There's a precedent in the defence forces for this. Major Glenn Todhunter was an Australian Army pilot who lost both his legs after a plane crash during a training flight. At first he was told he'd never fly again in the army. But after eight years of rebuilding his life and then fighting for his job back, he's now flying both rotary and fixed-wing aircraft, and is the first and only amputee aviator in the history of the Australian Defence Force. His motto is a good one: 'The only limits to living an extraordinary life are the limits we place upon ourselves.' So, just like him, I'm aiming high, and am determined to get there.

It's not even like I can't fly either. A mate who's a pilot took me up in a small plane recently and let me fly it – against his better judgement! It was awesome, being so weightless and carefree. By the end, I was doing 45-degree wing-dip turns.

I'm driving too. The boys from the diving branch held a charity auction and donated all the proceeds to helping me get on with my life. With half the money raised, I bought a car, a Lexus, which was very comfortable for me to drive. I had a knob installed on the steering wheel that spun around to make it easier for me to turn the wheel, although I find it quite easy to steer properly with one hand anyway. After a period of trial and error, I now tend to use my left leg on both the brake and accelerator. That works better than using the prosthetic.

The other half of the money I donated back to the welfare fund for clearance divers. I wanted to make sure that anyone else who had an accident would be as well cared for as I had been. Later on, I sold the Lexus and bought a 3-litre turbo-diesel HiLux 'truckosaurus'. The extra room would come in handy one day, I thought, when I learnt to surf again and had to take my surfboards around with me.

Even as the navy was putting me through all the tests, it wanted me to try out for the Paralympics. The defence forces were trying to organise a joint team with the Paralympians and they sent me up to Cairns to take part in a swim training camp with some of the world's Paralympic champions. It was a great experience, and I did well, but I told them my heart wasn't in it. I was 34 by then and the oldest competitor there was 25, and even he was thinking of retiring. They were all kids, with time on their hands, living in Canberra to attend the Australian Institute of Sport – and there was no way I wanted to go back to Canberra after spending my adolescence in that town.

Besides, swim training can be incredibly boring, going up and down a pool for four hours a day, chasing that never-ending blue line on the bottom. You have to do that training to make the qualifying times, and you attend special camps constantly, all in the hope of winning a gold medal. And that's great for those who want it but I feel like I've got so much more that I want to do. I grew up doing drills in the pool five times a week until I was 15 and, much as I love swimming, I'm too busy now.

After my speech to the kids from CanTeen, I was keen to do more public speaking. If my experience could help other people, especially children, I was all for it. The navy was good about that too. They were happy for me to do those kinds of speeches and, as long as I didn't appear in uniform or talk about the military, I no longer needed to ask for their permission.

I did a number of other charity speeches. One was for the Raize the Roof foundation, which was started in 2009 by an old Canberran mate of my brother Sean, Lincoln Dal Cortivo, and his sister, Danielle. They are raising money to buy a local block of land, build a house on it, and auction it off, with the proceeds going partly to an orphanage in Africa, and partly to sick kids in Australia. I called Oceanworld Manly where I'd done my dive with *60 Minutes* to ask if we could organise a shark dive to be auctioned off at the event to help bring in more cash. They were great about it and donated two tickets. On the night I did my presentation, and then they auctioned off the prize. But the highest bidder had other ideas. He said he'd double the money he was paying if I'd go and do it with him. I couldn't very well refuse, and it ended up making $1500 for the charity from that prize alone. And I did enjoy the shark dive more that second time!

Another day I did a talk for the crew of the warship *HMAS Newcastle*, apologising to them first for making them listen to a clearance diver speak about himself for an hour . . . I enjoyed that too. I just told them about how I managed, and why I wanted to stay in my job. By now I was regularly being asked to speak to all sorts of people about my life, what happened and how I got through it all. Even my old Canberra school, St Edmund's, asked me to come and make a speech to the students, which I thought was a little ironic. Walking back through those gates, being greeted warmly by the teachers, felt like such a different experience to the one I'd had when I was last there. And when I spoke to that assembly hall of 1200 kids, you could have heard a pin drop. It was awesome.

Audiences have all seemed to be interested in what I've got to say and I've got better as I've gone along. One time I bumped into Layne Beachley, the seven-time world-champion surfer, at a surf carnival in Manly. We became friendly, and she helped me a lot in my public speaking. She told me to let myself go a little bit more, and try to convey how I feel to an audience. I find that hard; I don't like talking about my feelings. She told me that showing your vulnerability can be a strength. I'm trying!

I'm also careful about whether or not to show an audience the photos of my injuries. Some people are really fascinated – especially by the teeth marks – but others find the images of the blood and torn flesh too confronting. If I'm not sure about my judgement, I've learned to tell people to look away if they're squeamish. I'm also talking to the navy staff about using that little piece of the video they took during our exercise, which shows the actual shark attack. I think people would love to see it. You can't see much detail, but it's still very dramatic.

It's funny, but after nearly every one of my speeches, when I invite questions, someone always puts their hand up or comes up to me to ask the same thing. No, not Nikes this time, but about the motto of improvise, adapt and overcome, and what it means to me. That's always easy to answer. As I look at how my life is now and what it might have been if I'd given up at the first hurdle, it means absolutely everything.

# 24

## SHARKS AND ME

People ask me all the time how I feel about sharks. Ironically, for someone who's been scared of them for just about all his life and who's suffered so much at the teeth of one, I now no longer have a fear of them. That day I was unlucky to be attacked, but the odds of something like that happening twice to the same person must be so extraordinarily high, I'd more or less be guaranteed a spot in the *Guinness World Records*.

Of course, I wish it hadn't happened. I can't pretend otherwise. But I've certainly ended up with a lot of opportunities I might otherwise never have had. As well as knowing I'll feature in every documentary that's ever made about sharks from now on, I've been happy to see the speaking engagements continue. Some of them, however, have been quite unexpected. One day I was asked to go to speak to some members of the naval treaty group for the

English-speaking countries – America, Britain, Canada, Australia and New Zealand, or ABCANZ for short – who were meeting at *HMAS Watson* in Sydney. After my talk, an officer from New Zealand approached me and asked if I'd be prepared to travel over the Tasman to address navy divers there about my experiences. I didn't hesitate. A few weeks later I received another phone call asking if I'd be interested in going to the US to speak at a navy working divers group. I was actually about to travel overseas to Japan and Thailand for a holiday with Kim – her first time out of Australia – and the dates looked as if they might clash. That didn't bother the guy at the other end of the phone.

'What if we fly you both over to San Diego from Japan and then fly you back again?' he asked. 'We'll show you a great time.'

And so it was that after spending a week in Japan, Kim and I flew to San Diego in May 2010 to meet up with the US divers working group. Over 225 divers were in attendance, including some from the marines, airforce, army and coastguard. After I'd talked about my work with the Australian clearance divers, told them the story about the shark attack and my recovery and then given a bit of a motivational presentation, they gave me a standing ovation. To have recognition like that from fellow divers in the US felt like a huge honour. They, apparently, felt much the same.

Kim kept saying how they were treating me like a rock star. There was an article about me, with a photo, in the next official newsletter for the divers of the US Navy. 'Paul has overcome this extraordinary experience with grace, perseverance, and a positive attitude,' it said. 'His story is one of motivation and inspiration, and it was an honor to have him share his story with us.' It seemed that wasn't the end of it, either. There were a few high-ranking naval officers there from Washington who approached me later and said they'd love to have me over to talk to members of their dive school in Florida in the future.

Afterwards, Kim and I flew back to Japan and then finished off our holiday in Thailand, where I got the tattoo on my left arm added to and extended down my arm and across my shoulder in the traditional bamboo style. It's a dragon with the words in Chinese script, 'Accomplish everything without fear'.

Being back among divers – from all countries – made me even more impatient to dive myself and, just before Australia Day 2010, an ex-clearance diver mate of mine from the SAS arrived back in Sydney and got in touch. He was taking a friend of his for his first dive and asked me if I wanted to go along. I thought that'd be awesome. Someone from the surf company Rip Curl Australia had seen those paparazzi photos of me in my old wetsuit and had called to offer to make me a new one that'd be tailored for my prosthetics, with a zip in the back of the leg. I'd said yes, and just received it. It looked good and I was dying to try it out. Slipping back into the water was a wonderful experience. I'd just got my waterproof leg by then, although I was still having a few problems with it. I knew it would take me a while to get my swimming speed up, but I wasn't too worried; I knew that would come.

It was incredible being deep in the ocean, doing what I love to do, and never even once fearing the presence of sharks. After all, if I were ever to be attacked again, the shark stood a decent chance of biting something very hard that'd definitely persuade him I'm not good to eat.

Later that afternoon I got together with a bunch of work-mates at the beach and one of them was out on a jet ski, towing a donut – an inflatable ring – behind him. A couple of the lads were having a go, sitting in the ring being flung around in the waves, and it looked like a lot of fun. I wanted a go, so I scrambled down the rocks, got in and jumped into the next incoming wave. At first, it was great. But my mate went faster and faster, hitting the waves harder and flipping me in different directions, and he suddenly made a sharp turn. The donut and I went one way, and my prosthetic leg flew off and went the other. I could hear Kim and the boys yelling and laughing from the apartment balcony where they were watching.

Lucky I was in a group of navy divers. Everyone immediately grabbed snorkels and masks and swam over to the spot where I'd lost the leg. We duck-dove the 9 metres down and searched the radius. Naturally, we found it pretty quickly. All that training would never go to waste.

All this time I was still working hard in the gym every day, with weights and plenty of cardio to build up to peak fitness. The day I bench-pressed 120 kilograms I knew I was well on my way. I'm still working on my chin-ups – my personal best is 23 at the moment – but push-ups I could keep going with all day. I took part in a charity race up Sydney Tower's 1504 stairs too. I didn't do too badly. The winner of the race was a German professional stair-runner who did it in 7 minutes and 4 seconds. I finished in 18 minutes and 55 seconds.

I take supplements to help me train harder and recover quicker and one of the sports supplements companies, Australian Sports

Nutrition, got in touch with me after they'd seen me wearing their 'Harden the Fuck Up' T-shirt on *60 Minutes*. They sent me some of their products to help me rebuild myself. I still use their proteins and pre-trainers to this day. I'm a strong believer in taking extra protein to aid the body repairing itself. It certainly helped me get my strength back. Out of the gym I like to do an hour or two of Wii boxing, which was instrumental to my recovery when I couldn't do any cardio. I put on one of the boxing games and bounce around the lounge on one leg with the second controller taped to the end of my arm. I told the people at my prosthetics company what I'd been doing with the Wii to aid my endurance and recovery, and the lady who conducted the rehabilitation there took my idea and created a program called WiiHab. I also swim, and am trying to strengthen my respiratory system by practising breath-hold swimming, or free diving as it's also known, in the pool at work with my waterproof leg and fins on. It's good practice in remaining calm and controlling your body, and not letting it control you. So far, I can swim 100 metres underwater without taking an extra breath. That's not bad.

In the old days I used to love running on the soft sand, which was always great for my fitness. Now I can get over the sand on my waterproof leg but it has its limitations with that non-bending knee. The shock-absorbing spring has still been known to rebound and fling me down the stairs when I use the wrong leg to step down. But with technology improving all the time and so many recent advances in prosthetics as a result of the Iraq and Afghanistan wars, I hope that it won't be long before I'll be back running along the beach.

I tried a waterproof arm for swimming too, but that didn't work so well. They gave me one with what looked like a paddle on the end, but it was more of a hindrance than anything else. I just prefer life without it and I'm still a pretty strong swimmer. I learned, when I trained with the Paralympians, to use the rest of my right arm as a paddle. The guy who was teaching us said we should use whatever we have as our tools. Those words have stayed with me.

I still really wanted to stand again on a surfboard and feel that amazing rush, and yet another opportunity came along with a new reality show on OneHD, *Manly Surf*, which was going to be about Manly Surf School and its instructors, presented by Layne Beachley. The producers contacted me and asked me if I'd be willing to have a surf lesson on camera for the program. They didn't have to ask twice; I was there. That day I was nervous I wouldn't be able to do it and I'd look like an idiot on camera, but after a couple of goes, much to my surprise, I was standing with my waterproof leg on the surfboard, racing over those waves. In the interview afterwards the producer said to me that I'd done well. I disagreed.

'Everyone has their struggles,' I replied. 'Some people don't have the balance. Some people don't have the fitness. I just don't have the leg!'

I'd been spending a lot of time with Kim, and she'd been great. We'd taken a break together in Queensland and were looking at the brochures of things to do while on holiday. There were some things I couldn't do, like ride a bicycle, so I started looking for something I could do instead. I found it immediately: skydiving.

Kim's scared of heights and said she didn't think they'd let me jump out of a plane. I said, 'If we go there and they let me, then you'll do it too, won't you?' She agreed, convinced there was no way I'd be allowed. But, of course, they said yes, and she ended up having to do it with me. She came diving with sharks with me too, and finished up complaining more about the temperature of the water than the sharks.

Kim also helped me move house again. I'd always loved Bondi but I wanted to get away from the crowds. I wasn't able to go for a walk outside without people staring. In a bar someone would often come up and say I was inspiring, which I told them I could only cope with if they bought me a beer. I found it a bit embarrassing, to be honest. But it'd got to the point where Kim said I should make up a T-shirt that said, 'Yes, I Am That Guy But I Don't Want To Talk About It'. I didn't much like going to the gym there either as I felt people were looking at me – despite Kim insisting they were looking only because I could do more chin-ups than them, but all the attention made me uncomfortable.

It was also pretty awkward whenever I wanted to go for a swim or a surf. For that, I needed to wear my waterproof leg, but to walk to the beach I'd have to use my regular C Leg. Things got tricky if I had to swap them over at the beach and leave one behind on the sand. Otherwise, I'd have to drive two seconds to the beach and swap in the car. So I decided I wanted to live close enough to the beach to walk over on my waterproof leg, but it'd have to be somewhere a bit more low-key. I looked everywhere and finally ended up in a ground-floor apartment on the northern beaches with a bit of grass outside. I ended up getting a dog, a ridgeback-cross-mastiff called Chip, from a rescue pound. I knew Kim was quite keen on moving in together, but I felt I needed some time on my own first, to really prove to myself I could cope.

We were still enjoying each other's company, and that trip away to Thailand and Japan, with the speech in San Diego in the middle, had been a blast. In the four weeks we'd only argued once and that had been at an airport when we were both tired and cranky. It was when we arrived back, however, that things came to a head. We wanted different things. I was keen just to see Kim a couple of days a week and have my own space the rest of the time, but she said that wasn't the kind of relationship she wanted. We argued and I called it quits. I had some of my stuff at her place, but she mailed it over to me, and then didn't respond to my texts or emails.

After about three months, I went over to Kim's flat one evening. I didn't think she'd buzz me in but apparently she'd been expecting her flatmate so hadn't looked to see who it was. When she opened the door, she went pale and asked me what I wanted. I said I needed to speak to her; I'd made a mistake and I wanted her back. When we'd returned from holiday, I'd felt under pressure to move in together but I hadn't been ready. Now I'd shown myself I could live alone, and re-established my independence without people around me all the time, but I'd found it wasn't as much fun without her. We'd built all these amazing memories together since she'd stood by me after the shark attack. I'd realised I didn't want to build new memories, I wanted to add to the ones we already had.

She said she'd have to think about it and made me sweat

on her decision for about a week before I met up with her with Chip's new baby sister, Bonnie, a mastiff-cross-boxer. I figured, who could resist me with a cute little puppy? By the end of the afternoon we'd got back together. We'd made plans to move in together.

Life now is good, and I like to present myself as Mr Invincible, but that's not to say there aren't problems or the occasional setback. It's still taking a while for the prosthetic updates to settle down, and as the muscles in the top of my leg atrophy, the socket has to keep being adjusted to fit properly. At one point I had three 3-millimetre socks over the bottom of my leg to make it fit, which wasn't ideal, especially not in summer! I've had a few mishaps with my hand too. The stronger upgrades are much more expensive but I'm holding out for the newer technology, which will enhance the usage and, in turn, my quality of life. My current hand breaks almost monthly, and once I managed to snap it completely in half in a car door. Often, I just prefer not to wear it as it can get in the way and just draws more attention to me.

The phantom pains are still there. Sometimes I might not get them for a few weeks, but then they'll hit hard and often continue for a while. During the day, they're not so bad because I'm constantly moving about and am generally preoccupied with something else. It's harder when I go to bed and I'm lying there and there's nothing else to think about. So, unlike the old days when I could sleep instantly whenever I wanted to, it can take me up to two hours to get to sleep. I now use a little ENAR machine, a handheld Electro-Neuro Adaptive Regulator, which stimulates the nerves to relieve pain. Hopefully, in time the pains will subside.

It's been nearly two years, though, so I've prepared my mind and body for life with them.

I can't pretend I *don't* have some dark times. There are moments when I still struggle with how I am right now. I just don't know if the navy will let me do everything I want to do. But if I leave the navy, who will hire me? I'm not qualified in anything else. All I'm trained in is soldiering, and who's going to hire a one-legged, one-armed soldier? Then I tell myself to get over it and move on.

The thing that's hit me the hardest, however, has been the number of subsequent operations I've had to undergo. I don't like to talk about them much as I don't want anything holding me back from getting on with my career. But just as I'm coming to grips with life, I have to have another op. So far, I've had to have no fewer than three to remove bone spurs, a growth formed as the body tries to repair itself by building extra bone. This can be difficult when it causes wear and tear or pain if it presses or rubs on other bones or tissue. One op was just before I went overseas with Kim. Dr Ho recommended three weeks' recovery but, by the end of the second week, I was actually sightseeing, walking for eight hours a day – although in a lot of pain. I couldn't bear to allow it to slow me down. The latest one, in November 2010, I hope will be my last, with the doc removing three spurs and blasting the bone with radiation to stop the problem recurring.

On the way to the hospital I always play the same little game. Once I'm hooked up to the IV and the heart-rate monitor, I deliberately try to relax and calm myself to lower my heart rate enough to set off the alarm. I used to do it all the time after the shark attack just to see the nurses come running. Maybe I couldn't move, but that didn't mean I couldn't have some fun. There's never enough time on the way into surgery though – before you know it, the anaesthetist is pulling out the needle and telling you it might sting. This is the second part of the game: trying to stay awake. It's a very short game, however, and I've yet to come anywhere close to a win.

The last time I was in I was expected to stay at least overnight but as soon as I woke, I checked that I didn't have a drain in my leg, then got dressed and left the ward on my crutches, with Kim carrying my prosthetic leg while the nurse raced around trying to stop me. Dr Ho stressed that I needed three weeks again with absolutely no walking but he let slip once that he always adds an extra week for my recovery because he knows I always cut it short . . .

You have to find the positives in everything. At the beginning of 2011 I went over to Abu Dhabi with Kim to visit my dad. While I was there, my limitations came back to haunt me. I decided I'd better not try to ride a camel, and when others ran up sand dunes in the middle of a trip into the desert, I couldn't join in. That really, really affects me. It hurts me that I can't do those things. Later, in Dubai, we visited a ski slope, and while I'd have loved to do some snowboarding, I had my walking leg on so it just wasn't possible. The next day we went to a water park. I'd been looking forward to getting in the water but, when I went into the changing rooms to put my waterproof leg on, the locking system seized up and it wouldn't snap on. After 40 minutes of struggling with it, I came out and said to Kim it was hopeless, I couldn't go in the water.

Despite being so upbeat most of the time, I do have to face the fact that there are some things I'll never be able to do as well as I could before. But we had a great time in Abu Dhabi and it was good to spend some time with Dad. One day we went out with him and his girlfriend and towards the end of the day, I grabbed him and said, 'Look, Dad, I've never told you this before, but I love you and I'm proud of you and I'm very happy you're happy.' I gave him a hug. And then we went on drinking.

I guess this whole thing has brought me a bit closer to all of my family. I tend to speak to, and see, my mum a bit more often. My brothers and sister are all busy with their own lives and are often away with the army but it's good when we can catch up. Jacqui, who served as a medic on the frontline in Afghanistan, and is now a corporal, was given a Commendation for Distinguished Service in the 2011 honours. I'm really proud of her. She's grown into a very strong woman mentally and she's making the most out of her life and not watching it go idly by. Obviously, they don't just hand these awards out like Tim Tams so she must be doing some pretty special stuff. I'm very proud.

As for my day-to-day life, things go on as normal – or as close to it as I can make possible. My injuries used to be a great excuse for not cleaning up in the kitchen after I cooked, but Kim didn't believe me when I told her the battery in my arm was flat. It made me laugh when Kim sometimes played what she called my 'shark boy card' when, for instance, she knew I'd like a better table at a restaurant, where people couldn't stare. Sadly, though, our relationship didn't make it through. I guess I'm still a bit shy about commitment, but I'll always be grateful to her for everything she did for me. I feel like I've not only lost my girlfriend, but also one of my best friends.

Yet I still have plenty of things to keep me busy. One day I was asked to model underpants for a mate of mine who's brought out a range called The Navy Diver. Six hours of flexing my muscles and trying to look good for those photos wasn't anywhere near as hard as a pack march but it was bloody embarrassing. I'm always looking for other projects I can do too. I'm now into designing a series of T-shirts, based on the roles I've had in the military and using photography from my own collection and those taken by mates on military operations around the globe. It's fun, and who knows what might happen one day.

I still also dream of riding a motorbike again; like with diving, it makes you feel completely free. After the shark attack, it took me ages to agree to sell my beautiful Italian sports bike. I didn't want to let it go. People would call up about it and I'd tell them it'd already been sold. But now I've finally sold it to a mate and am in the process of buying a Harley-Davidson because its sitting position will be easier with my robot leg. I'll have the bike modified to suit me and while I'll be able to ride it on a track, I don't yet know how I'll get a licence to ride it on the road. It's my next challenge, and I just can't wait.

**Kim**

It's Paul's sheer determination to tackle each challenge that astonishes me. He always wants to get the kind of things done that let him have his old life back, when he could do anything. He'll be cooking and having a problem with cling wrap or the can opener, but he always manages and finds a way. With the car, for instance, he worked out that it's easier to start it by leaning in and turning the ignition with his left hand and then getting in, instead of leaning over to do it when he's already sitting in the driver's seat.

The bike is the most heartbreaking thing for him at the moment. Sitting in traffic, watching bikes zoom up the inside lane – you see him roll his eyes and grip the wheel in frustration. I know he will get there one day. He's thinking of a Harley and will probably have one by the end of the year, knowing what he's like.

I am so proud of how much he challenges himself every day. It has definitely made me a better person too. I don't feel I have the right to complain about the small stuff like getting out of bed in the mornings when he has to hop to the bathroom, then spend the first ten minutes putting on his leg before getting on with his day – but he does it, and doesn't ever complain.

He is very strong in both mind and body and I love him to bits!

Looking back over the last couple of years since I was attacked by that shark, I think it's fair to say that it's cost me an awful lot – physically, emotionally, psychologically, in every way, really. Considering that, however, I think I've always been pretty fair to sharks. After my encounter, a lot of people kept calling for them to be culled, to clear them out of the sea. My argument is always that the sea is their domain; we're the ones trespassing in their territory. Just because you get bitten by a dog, that's no argument to kill all dogs, and if you get hit by a car, that doesn't mean you should pull all cars off the road. We have to be reasonable. Even so, it was a strange day when I received an email from a US-based organisation called the Pew Environment Group, an independent, not-for-profit body funded by a number of charities with a commitment 'to improve society'. Their think-tank, a leading member of the Shark Alliance, a coalition of non-government organisations dedicated to restoring and conserving shark populations around the world, was putting on an event in New York to apply pressure on the UN to protect sharks – and they wanted me to and represent Australia be one of their star speakers.

While one of the species had done its best to have me for breakfast, it seems they are under great threat. An estimated 73 million sharks are killed every year for shark fin soup, and while they've roamed our oceans since before the age of dinosaurs, finning and overfishing have left nearly a third of all shark species threatened with extinction. We can't blame them when they attack us; it's their nature to hunt. But, it seemed to me, we humans really should know better. I happily agreed to go to New York.

I was unsure what to expect, but the organisers were incredibly well-prepared and welcoming. I met a host of other shark-attack survivors, made my speech to a room of delegates from a variety of countries and spent two and a half days straight giving interviews for print, TV and radio outfits from around the world. I even did a morning-show spot on US TV. The more I heard, the more I felt such a movement was absolutely necessary. You take the sharks out of the ecosystem and suddenly the whole system is skewed. Shark conservation is just a bite-sized chunk, but a very important bite-sized chunk, of what needs to be done to look after the environment generally.

Afterwards, I told the group I'd be happy to talk about shark protection again. There are times, of course, when I curse the shark that, in just a few mad seconds, completely altered the course of my life. But then if it hadn't been a shark, it might have been that dog who mauled me when I was younger, any one of my many motorbike crashes, a stray bullet in the army or, with clearance divers now deployed in Afghanistan to dispose of Improvised Explosive Devices and unexploded ordnances, any incendiary device.

I sometimes look back and think I was predetermined to fall in harm's way, whether by choice or by career. I always chose not to live on the safe side, to live large, to take risks, to push the envelope time after time. I just ended up in the wrong place at the wrong time, but what didn't kill me certainly made me stronger.

I've also learnt a lot about mental strength. I've come to real-ise that, without motivation, goals can remain pipe dreams. You need to care about and really want a certain outcome and then pour your heart and soul into achieving it. I've seen in others, and learnt myself, that the human body can endure more and perform better than we might ever give it credit for. But it's not the body working alone. The body is just the nail being driven in; the mind is the hammer, the driving force that will push a person far beyond their own expectations and on to success. I think what stops other people is that they fear the act instead of focusing on the outcome.

Only occasionally does my mind let go and I catch myself thinking, *What if?* But then I give myself a mental upper-cut and say 'Fuck that!' I can't go down that road. There's no point. Life is here to be lived. And with the right attitude and willingness to deal with the hurdles, it really can be bloody awesome.

# POSTSCRIPT

**Vice Admiral Russ Crane, Chief of Navy**

When word came through that there had been a shark attack on one of our own, I must confess that I feared the worst. Quick thinking and good training by Paul's fellow dive-team members saved his life but the outcome was always going to be difficult.

In the days following the attack, I visited Paul in hospital and met a remarkable young man. Despite the obviously shocking nature of his injuries, it was just as clear to me that de Gelder was a sailor of true resolve. Whereas most of us may have been tempted to succumb to shock, pain, depression, and perhaps even self-pity, Paul was having none of that. He made it crystal clear to me that he had no intention of giving up. His focus was on the future.

Since that time, I am pleased to say that Paul de Gelder has lived up to my first impressions. As I write this, we cannot yet say exactly what the future holds. Paul's rehabilitation has been long and gruelling but nothing short of inspirational.

Determination in the face of adversity is a trait those of us who wear the navy uniform hold dear. Paul's determination and focus from the week we met to this present day should be an example to us all.

### Commander Michael Egan, United States Navy, Supervisor of Diving

Paul de Gelder has an incredible story to tell. It is a story of overwhelming odds, brilliantly overcome through hard work, gutsy determination and a great sense of humour. I knew in an instant that I needed Paul to tell his story to the divers of the United States Navy. His effortless charm and engaging manner reels you in for the most motivating ride of your life. A man is not defined by what happens to him, he is defined by how he handles it. That makes Paul a most remarkable man!

### Petty Officer Clearance Diver Lane Patterson (Patto), Paul's supervisor

I'm constantly astonished by how Paul handled the attack and by what he's done since.

His attitude . . . I've never seen any negativity at all. I expected there'd be some kind of post-accident depression, since he lost two limbs and was such an active person. But I've not seen anything like that at all. Maybe he's felt some dark moments at night when he's been by himself, but to everyone else he's been nothing but upbeat and thankful. There's never been any, 'Why was I in the water?'

Instead, he's been completely inspiring. When I was in Afghanistan a little while later, I had a lot of trauma and terrible incidents where I could have easily been badly hurt. But if I had, if I'd lost a leg or arm or eye, I never would have had the guts to feel sorry for myself after being around Paul. I wouldn't be game. I think that goes for the other guys too.

He's made the best of a situation that probably would have destroyed someone else.

**Commander Ashley Shanks, Paul's boss**

I'm so impressed by how positive Paul is. He's become almost a life coach to the other guys in the way he connects with everyone. He's a real asset. He's got such a great spirit.

**Layne Beachley, former professional surfer and the first woman in history to win seven surfing world championships, six of them consecutively**

I got to know Paul at the launch of the TV show *Manly Surf*, where he was learning to surf again with only one leg. I have an enormous amount of respect for him. Like most of Australia, I'd seen him on TV as a result of the shark attack, and heard about the challenges he faced. I felt he was so heroic. He's so strong-willed and stubborn, and so matter-of-fact about his experience. I wanted to get to know him a bit better to see what makes him tick, and how someone like him was able to overcome an experience that the rest of us wouldn't wish on our worst enemy. I admired him.

After a while, I got to see the softer side of the tough guy. To overcome such serious challenges as he's had, or to achieve, you need to be hard-headed and driven, but there's always a softer side to everyone like that. There's also power and strength in vulnerability and it's important to show that part of yourself, especially in public life.

I draw a lot of inspiration from him. He's an incredibly determined human being. But he's also very gregarious and fun to be around. And, of course, he's a great surfer – for someone who's only got one leg!

## Dr Kevin Ho, plastic, reconstructive and cosmetic surgeon

He's very inspirational from a personal point of view. He has enormous spirit, and his mindset and training, everything that made him who he was before, helped him after the attack. He saw problems simply as hurdles to overcome.

I won't be surprised if he ends up going on to even bigger things than he was destined for before the shark attack. I've always got time for Paul and am really proud of him.

Whatever he goes on to achieve in the future, the most important thing about him is his wonderful attitude. If we look at what his life would have been before this, maybe he wouldn't have achieved everything he's achieving now.

## Tony Grabs, director of trauma services at Sydney's St Vincent's Hospital

Paul's a very remarkable man who has a character as strong as an ox. He's shown a skill-set that would match anyone in the world in the situation he was in. I don't think I ever saw him get down about what had happened, which is astonishing. He lifts the spirits of everyone around him. I'm proud that we have Australians like this in our country.

**Pat de Gelder, mum**

He's astounded us by what he's done. Paul's never, ever whinged and is always so positive about life and is a wonderful person to be around.

**Jacqui de Gelder, sister**

Whenever people hear my name, they ask me if I'm Paul's sister. I think it's fantastic how well he's coped. As an army medic, I see a lot of people whingeing about stuff every day, trying to get off work. My brother has one leg and one arm and yet he's fitter than me, so stop bitching! He's very strong and has great willpower.

**Steve Dalla Costa (Dalla), friend**

After the attack, I remember several of our friends saying if this happened to anyone other than de Gelder, they'd probably be dead. I think they're right. Now, whenever any of Paul's friends are having a bad day, we all think of him and are instantly buoyed. He's created a different perspective on life for us all.

**Able Seaman Mark Hudson (Huddo), friend**

He's an inspirational guy. He's always had his head screwed on, and you have a genuine conversation with him about things of substance. He's handled everything incredibly, and he really drives himself forward. He's still living life to its fullest.

## Glenn Orgias, surfer who lost his hand to a shark at Bondi the day after Paul

I don't think I'd have been able to face up to losing my hand in the same way if it wasn't for Paul. Having him around made the whole situation easier because of his positive attitude and the way he leads by example. Seeing him surfing in Bondi was what got me back into the ocean. I know he's also inspired a lot of other folk to overcome hard times. He'll do great things, whatever he puts his mind to.

## Peter Overton, reporter, *60 Minutes*

From the moment I met Paul in his hospital bed, I knew I was privileged. He was horrendously mauled and recovering from such drastic surgery, and I was overwhelmed by his aura, his positive outlook and his will to live. In eight years of reporting for *60 Minutes*, Paul, without question, is one of the most inspirational human beings I have met! Everyone, whoever they are, can learn so much from Paul – I know I have.

## Kim Elliott, former girlfriend

If we could bottle his positivity, we could sell it for a million dollars. He struggles to see why others aren't as positive. He doesn't understand why others can't get up at 6 a.m. and go to the gym before work. 'Why not?' he asks, genuinely puzzled. And he doesn't see himself as anything special! Yet he is truly amazing. His physical and mental strength have got him through this life-threatening ordeal, and I love him more than anything, and always will.

# ACKNOWLEDGMENTS

I could easily write another entire book about the amazing people who have played a role in my life and, more specifically, helped me to endure since that morning in February 2009.

To the men who kept me alive – Leading Seaman Jeremy Thomas, Able Seaman Ryan Dart, Able Seaman Arthur McLachlin and Petty Officer Lane Patterson – without your fast action and steel under pressure, I have no doubt that I'd have been dead before we hit the wharf.

Thank you to my friends and family who rushed to my hospital bed and vigilantly stood by me, feeding me positivity and information. Without your help that pit that is fear and despair would have been far harder to climb out of. I love you all.

Thank you to the amazing paramedics, doctors and nurses at St Vincent's Hospital, especially my surgeons Dr Tony Grabs and Dr Kevin Ho. You have a wonderful gift of improving the quality of people's lives but hopefully I'll never be lying in front of you again.

Thank you to Simon and Kerrie from Australian Sports Nutrition and Shane from ASN Neutral Bay for fuelling my passion and love of training with your support and not least of all, your supplements. Thanks also to Rip Curl for my two new wetsuits, and to David Christie for taking all the stress and paperwork out of dealing with the Department of Veteran Affairs.

Thank you to my agent, Selwa Anthony, who gives me friendship and guidance, not to mention a fantastic Lebanese feed whenever she can. Thanks too to Sue Williams who helped me with my story and my publisher at Penguin, Andrea McNamara, for wanting me to tell it.

Without the support of the men and women of the Royal Australian Navy, my mates in the Royal Australian Infantry and especially the Clearance Diving branch, my life would be far less fulfilled. Thank you for working behind the scenes and on the front line of my life to support me and get me back to what I love: Navy diving.

Thank you to everyone for their kind words and messages on blogs, Facebook and email, and in interviews and articles. I'm not sure what it is that I'm doing, but it seems to be making a difference for the better in people's lives, so I'll just keep going.

Thank you to my childhood friend Brock who gave up his job and time to move in and look after me when I couldn't do it myself. You are far stronger than you believe.

Finally, to the beautiful Kim. Thank you for standing by me

strong during a time when others would have wanted to bolt. You always make me feel like the most amazing man in the world and you'll always be in my heart.